Joyce Rodgers
FatAL
Distractions #538
2.00
07

D0967325

Letters from HOME

TED HAGGARD

Letters from HOME,

TED HAGGARD

Regal

From Gospel Light
Ventura, California, U.S.A.

Published by Regal Books
From Gospel Light
Ventura, California, U.S.A.
Printed in the U.S.A.

Regal Books is a ministry of Gospel Light, an evangelical Christian publisher dedicated to serving the local church. We believe God's vision for Gospel Light is to provide church leaders with biblical, user-friendly materials that will help them evangelize, disciple and minister to children, youth and families.

It is our prayer that this Regal book will help you discover biblical truth for your own life and help you meet the needs of others. May God richly bless you.

For a free catalog of resources from Regal Books/Gospel Light, please call your Christian supplier or contact us at 1-800-4-GOSPEL *or* www.regalbooks.com.

Cover and interior design by Robert Williams
Edited by Christi Goeser

LIBRARY OF CONGRESS CATALOGING-IN-PUBLICATION DATA
Haggard, Ted.
    Letters from home/Ted Haggard.
       p. cm.
    ISBN 0-8307-2528-8 (hardcover)
    ISBN 0-8307-3058-3 (paperback)
       1. Teenagers—Religious life. 2. Teenagers—Conduct of life. I. Title

    BV4531.3 .H34 2002
    248.8'34—dc21   2001048811

1 2 3 4 5 6 7 8 9 10 11 12 13 14 15 / 09 08 07 06 05 04 03 02

Rights for publishing this book in other languages are contracted by Gospel Light Worldwide, the international nonprofit ministry of Gospel Light. Gospel Light Worldwide also provides publishing and technical assistance to international publishers dedicated to producing Sunday School and Vacation Bible School curricula and books in the languages of the world. For additional information, visit www.gospellightworldwide.org; write to Gospel Light Worldwide, P.O. Box 3875, Ventura, CA 93006; or send an e-mail to info@gospellightworldwide.org.

CONTENTS

Introduction 9

Letter 1 11
Live As If There Are No Secrets

Letter 2 23
Fear God, Not People

Letter 3 37
Realize How Much God Values You

Letter 4 51
Acknowledge God in a Pagan Culture

Letter 5 65
Cooperate with the Holy Spirit

Letter 6 81
Maintain Power Under Pressure

Letter 7 97
Become Rich Toward God

Letter 8 113
Seek the Kingdom of God

Letter 9 125
Be Dressed and Ready to Serve God

Letter 10 143
Understand the Consequences of Your Beliefs

Letter 11 155
Discern the Times

Letter 12 169
Learn to Manage Conflict

INTRODUCTION

My wife, Gayle, and I have five children: Christy (19), Marcus (17), Jonathan (14), Alex (11) and Elliot (8). Jonathan, Alex and Elliot are all going to be home for many more years, but Christy and Marcus are at the ages when college, careers and marriage are looming near. Before we know it, our only daughter and our oldest son will be raising families of their own—and I'll be writing books on being a grandparent!

In Colorado, during the winter, parents often go into Super Protection Mode when the kids get ready to go outside. "Do you have your coat? Do you have your gloves? Make sure you grab that fleece vest!" If they're old enough to drive, you make sure the tank has plenty of gas, that they know how to use four-wheel drive and that there is a flashlight, blanket and cell phone for emergencies. You know that probably nothing will go wrong, but you want them to be prepared for anything that could come their way.

Christy and Marcus are both getting ready to "go outside" figuratively and literally as they pursue college, internships and job offers. And though I know that they are strong, capable and resilient people who will have success in everything they do, I want them to be prepared. I want them to have a clear path to follow and to be protected from the storms of life, because I am their dad.

The letters in this book are for Christy and Marcus, and they are also for anyone else who is traveling on the road of life—which means *all* of us. So parents, don't wait! Instill these biblical truths into the hearts of your kids—even as early as the preteen years. It will help them get a jump on the game! Each letter is based on an idea from Luke 12, a chapter in the Bible where Jesus addresses so many of the key principles that determine the degree of success that we enjoy in life. In this chapter, Jesus discusses self-image, money, how to treat other people, how to think about the future, leadership, managing conflict and many other issues. I believe that Luke 12 is one of the most important chapters in the Bible; it is one that can help us develop a road map we can use to navigate the trickiest situations in life.

Christy, Marcus and everyone else reading these letters: I hope that you enjoy them and that they provide timely answers and assistance. I love Jesus' teaching so much, and I firmly believe that He intended for us to apply it to our lives and use it to build strength, security and happiness for us and everyone around us.

LIVE AS IF THERE ARE NO SECRETS

January 29

Dear Christy and Marcus,

The other day, as I was reading my Bible, I came across Luke 12. It's phenomenal! I've probably read Jesus' teachings in those verses hundreds of times, but it never captured my attention in this way until now. As I read, big ideas leapt off the page. This letter is filled with wonderful principles that each of us could apply to become better, more successful people. Jesus' teaching is so clear and refreshing, and it relates to every facet of our lives.

So, I decided to write you about each idea to help guide and direct you into the wonderful life that God desires for you. You're both getting nearer to finishing your education, and the most exciting decisions lie just ahead. But the principles in these letters won't just relate to your lives right now—these are simple, profound, overarching ideas that can guide you for the rest of your lives.

As a pastor, I've been able to watch how thousands of people live their lives. I've seen people with great potential ruin their lives with poor decisions, while others with less potential made strong decisions and became very successful. The lesson is simple: *The decisions you make each day will determine the course of your life.* If you choose to trust God and seek Him, your life will be much more secure and successful than if you trust yourselves and try to live life for yourselves.

Remember the other day when we talked about how some of your friends are suffering because their parents are divorcing or have made embarrassing decisions? I don't think we need to live this way. I think every one of us can make decisions that will open doors of life and hope. I believe that you were chosen from birth and have been called by God to live incredible lives and be a source of strength for other people.

Actually, you two are already a source of strength. I can see it in your friends when they come over to our home. They see you as stable, consistent people. They trust you. When they have no idea what their own parents are doing, they know that our home is a safe place. They can depend on the fact that there is security and love here. They can tell that no one is nervous or deceptive. They can tell that you are comfortable, and that gives them strength and hope. The atmosphere that we create and the atmosphere of our home didn't develop by itself. We all made intentional decisions to have a peaceful, strong, stable home. Remember, the decisions we make each day determine the course of our lives.

Your roles as sources of strength are only going to grow. In the coming years, you will see your friends choose to do all kinds of questionable things, but you don't have to make the same mistakes they do. Some of your friends will be in sexual trouble. Others will become discouraged, distracted or lazy and will fail to complete their educations. Others will forfeit their lives because of their lack of self-control and may lose themselves in drugs and alcohol. Some will sacrifice their closest relationships over foolish things and find themselves feeling lonely as they grow older.

You don't have to fall into any of these traps. I want you to be complete and satisfied with good things. Growing well is a skill, and to do it you need a strong spiritual life, a solid education and to be surrounded with loyal, lifelong friends.

But to get there, a few key principles from Luke 12 must be integrated into your lives. These principles will serve you all of your lives. You can trust them. They will never betray you.

The first of these principles is:

LIVE AS IF THERE ARE NO SECRETS.

Jesus introduced this idea in Luke 12 when He said,

There is nothing concealed that will not be disclosed, or hidden that will not be made known. What you have said in the dark will be heard in the daylight, and what you have whispered in the ear in the inner rooms will be proclaimed from the roofs (vv. 2-3).

Here is the basic idea: Everything in your life is public. There are no secrets. Everything you say, everything you do, everyplace you go, every thought you think is going to be known by all. So, if you want to do something that you'll have to keep secret, don't do it. If you want to say something that you'll have to ask people to keep secret, don't say it. Don't believe the lie that you can ever say something, do something, go somewhere or think things that others won't know about. People who believe in secrets are people who ultimately fail.

Think of people who tried to keep something secret. Richard Nixon thought no one would ever know about Watergate, but that's the only thing most Americans know about him. Jimmy Swaggart thought no one would ever know about his meeting with women other than his wife, but now people will always remember.

Today's biggest headlines are stories about people who thought they were doing something that was secret: Jesse Jackson's *secret* girlfriend and child, Monica Lewinski's *private* meetings with the president and *confidential* girl talk with Linda Tripp. Just think of the news stories we've watched together on television: Madalyn Murray O'Hair and her children's bodies found decomposing on a Texas farm; arms dealers and cop killers getting arrested; investigations into the poorly constructed buildings that crumbled so easy and killed so many thousands of people during the earthquakes in Turkey and India. In all of these stories, someone thought they were keeping secrets. Now their secrets are international news.

Today in *USA Today* there is an article about a bus driver who died suddenly while driving a school bus carrying 33 high school athletes, cheerleaders and two coaches. It makes me wonder if the driver's poor eating habits and lack of exercise became a public hazard. His private life might be the thing that tragically affected many people in his community. Did he overeat? Did he exercise? Did he stay up too late at night watching TV? Did a private habit of his end up costing people their lives? Yesterday, his thoughts about health were private; today they are in *USA Today*.

Another article in *USA Today* tells about the best-kept secret in the restaurant business. Years ago, Colonel Harland Sanders's secret recipe for chicken launched one of the great fried chicken franchises in the world. Now a judge has to make a decision for Kentucky Fried Chicken to ensure that the recipe stays a secret. Some time ago, a married couple bought a house from Colonel Sanders, and they found an old book in the attic that had the famous recipe written in it. They've come public with news of the recipe now, and KFC wants it back. KFC may win the battle for a little while, but even if this recipe is concealed or isn't really the right one, in the end everyone will know the formula for Kentucky Fried Chicken.

I'm laughing as I write this example, because I know that you, Christy, wouldn't be caught dead at KFC, and you, Marcus, could care less about a chicken recipe! But don't miss the point: There are no secrets. Everything that is hidden will be revealed—even fried chicken recipes.

One of my favorite stories about this is in Genesis 39, the story of Joseph and Potiphar's wife. Potiphar was a top official in the most powerful nation on Earth at the time, Egypt. Joseph was one of his hired servants. He was given the high position of being Potiphar's attendant and was in charge of everything at the house. Joseph was a teenager at the time, and the Bible says that he was "well-built and handsome" (v. 6).

It wasn't long before Potiphar's wife took notice of Joseph and tried to seduce him. Get the picture here: Joseph had the opportunity to develop a relationship with one of the most powerful women in the world. She had money, influence and the ability to arrange a very successful life for Joseph. I'm sure the thoughts that went through his mind were the same thoughts that go through everyone's mind when they are contemplating doing the wrong thing:

1.   *No one will ever know.*
This, without a doubt, was the situation here. They were alone in the house, and no one needed to find out. But this is always a lie. You can count on it. Every time you hear that thought in your head or have someone tell you "Let's do it—no one will ever find out," you can be sure that whatever you're considering is not worth doing.

2.   *I'll only do it this one time.*
This is the powerful lie that ruins so many people. I'll only have sex one time with this person. I'll only get drunk once. I'll only take one pill. I'll only take this money one time because I need it

so much, but I'm really not a thief. When people believe this, they start down a road they won't be able to come back from. One lie, one drink, one rendezvous, one pill, one joint, one look, one time. Yeah! Sure! Really? I don't think so.

Joseph could have thought that. No one will ever know, and I'll just do it once. It will be fun. It will feel good, and this lady will help me get my freedom, wealth and a life of luxury. If Joseph had thought that way, history would have been changed.

I know what you are thinking: *But he's just one guy. He was only a teenager in a foreign country. How could one slipup mean that much?* Well, it could, and the same dynamic is true for you. We are reading about Joseph thousands of years after the fact because he knew how to make good decisions. If you make good decisions, people could be reading about you thousands of years from now because you broke out of the crowd by being people of honor and wisdom.

But the primary person I want you to notice is Potiphar's wife. When she propositioned Joseph, the Bible says that he replied,

> With me in charge . . . my master does not concern himself with anything in the house; everything he owns he has entrusted to my care. No one is greater in this house than I am. My master has withheld no thing from me except you, because you are his wife. How then could I do such a wicked thing and sin against God? (vv. 8-9).

The Bible says she kept speaking to Joseph about going to bed with her day after day, but he refused to go to bed with her or even be alone with her. Then it got mean:

> One day [Joseph] went into the house to attend to his duties, and none of the household servants was inside.

She caught him by his cloak and said, "Come to bed with me!" But he left his cloak in her hand and ran out of the house (vv. 11-12).

When she saw that he had left his cloak in her hand and had run out of the house, she called her household servants.

"Look," she said to them, "this Hebrew has been brought to us to make sport of us! He came in here to sleep with me, but I screamed. When he heard me scream for help, he left his cloak beside me and ran out of the house" (vv. 14-15).

She kept his cloak beside her until Potiphar came home. Then she told him the story. Potiphar burned with anger and had Joseph put in prison.

As far as we know from the biblical account, Potiphar's wife lived her life, died and was buried thinking that everyone believed her story. She lived believing that there is such a thing as a secret, and she was wrong. Here we are, thousands of years later, laughing at this married woman who was chasing a teenage boy around her house trying to seduce him. Joseph's integrity and honor are intact, and Potiphar's wife is a mockery. She thought she had a secret, but there are no secrets. We all know.

Sometimes when I'm counseling a married couple, the husband and wife will come in to see me separately. At times, the woman will come in and tell me about her husband, and then the husband will come in and talk with me about secrets in his life that "no one knows." Little does he realize that his wife just told me everything in detail, and has probably been telling her friends as well. He's the only one who believes his secrets are secret.

This is also the case with parents and children. Every parent I know understands some things about their children that their children think are secrets, but the parents would never say anything because they don't want to embarrass their children. Likewise, kids know things about their parents that the parents believe are totally private, but the kids keep it quiet out of respect.

It's true with the police and citizens, employers and employees, and friends and family members. People know what's going on with other people. So, we are wise if we live our lives as if there are no secrets. If we have nothing to hide, then there's nothing for people to discover, and we're clean. Living as if there is no such thing as a secret will keep you from all kinds of pain and suffering, and it will open the door for you to receive God's love more fully. Live as if there is nothing to hide and you will maintain innocence.

The no-secrets principle works in our favor in more ways than one. God sees everything done in secret, both good and bad. Jesus once explained to His disciples that the good we do "in secret" will eventually be rewarded in public. When He talked about giving to others, He said,

> So when you give to the needy, do not announce it with trumpets, as the hypocrites do in the synagogues and on the streets, to be honored by men. I tell you the truth, they have received their reward in full. But when you give to the needy, do not let your left hand know what your right hand is doing, so that your giving may be in secret. Then your Father, who sees what is done in secret, will reward you (Matt. 6:2-4).

Some Bible translations say, "will reward you *openly* (emphasis added)."

In other words, if you serve God faithfully in secret, God won't keep it secret for long. If you do things just so other people will notice, God will not reward you. But if you do good works just because they are good and because you want to obey

God, He will reward you publicly. Jesus said the same principle applies to praying and fasting (see Matt. 6:5-18).

Interesting, isn't it, that the things that go on in a private room will be rewarded or punished openly? I think the reason is that God wants us to live lives of *integrity*. When something has integrity, it is whole, complete; it is the same without as it is within. When we live as if there is no such thing as a secret, our private lives and our public lives compliment one another—we are whole, complete. God wants us to accept the fact that everything we do matters, whether we're in public or alone.

Some will argue this point. But major leaders have lost their positions of influence because of what they did alone in a room. Our lives are to a large extent the product of our decisions. This is the theme of the entire book of Proverbs—really, it's one of the dominant themes of the whole Bible. Yesterday I came across some verses in Galatians 6 which said:

Do not be deceived: God cannot be mocked. A man reaps what he sows. The one who sows to please his sinful nature, from that nature will reap destruction; the one who sows to please the Spirit, from the Spirit will reap eternal life. Let us not become weary in doing good, for at the proper time we will reap a harvest if we do not give up (vv. 7-9).

Do you see? This idea echoes throughout the Bible. Our choices matter, and our lives are greatly impacted by the kinds of choices we make, either good or bad.

Of course, I'm not just talking about physical actions. Choices of the heart matter, too. Even the most personal things like holding a grudge or nurturing resentment end up affecting our lives in a dynamic way. You would think that whether we forgive someone or not would be a personal matter. But Jesus says,

> For if you forgive men when they sin against you, your heavenly Father will also forgive you. But if you do not forgive men their sins, your Father will not forgive your sins (Matt. 6:14-15).

I want you to have this idea firmly planted in your minds and applied in your lives. Once you understand that there is no such thing as a secret, your lives will be protected, and the lives of those who love and trust you will be strengthened.

Christy and Marcus, please don't ever fall into the trap of believing that you can do something in secret, even when you are far away from home. So many times, I've seen men and women get into trouble when they travel away from home because they believe that no one will ever know what they do when away. This is a lie, and it will always come back to haunt you.

In Genesis 38, the Bible tells the story of Judah, who went on a business trip. When he arrived at a distant town, he saw a prostitute and approached her to sleep with her. But he didn't have any money to pay her, so he had to give her some personal items as a down payment. Of course, everyone knew those items belonged to him, and soon what he had done in secret, far away from home, was a public matter. And, again, we're reading about his hypocrisy thousands of years later. His actions have brought shame to his entire family for many generations. It's just not worth it.

I remember an old tent preacher saying,

- sin will take you further than you want to go;
- cost you more than you want to pay;
- and keep you longer than you want to stay.

Of course, there's a lot of debate about what constitutes sin, but here's a simple definition: Sin is missing God's best plan for your life. It's disobedience to God's plan and the implementation of your own plan. It's wrong, and it always falls short.

I know that you have made a decision in your heart to live for God and find His best for your lives. But how will the world, or the enemy of our lives, steal from you and get you thrown off course? What scheme will the enemy of your lives use to control your lives? He will try to get you to keep a secret. If Richard Nixon didn't believe in secrets, we might see him as one of the greatest presidents in American history. If Bill Clinton didn't believe in secrets, he wouldn't have established a personal reputation of immorality and deceit. If you decide that you will live your lives as if there are no secrets, you will find yourself saying no to ungodliness and yes to the things that will make your lives strong and solid (see Titus 2:11-12).

Deciding to live as if there is no such thing as a secret is one of the greatest choices you could make in your entire lives. God loves you and has a wonderful plan for your life. He is good, and He wants the best for you. There is no reason not to trust Him and seek His perfect plan for you. To find His perfect plan for you is to live the highest life you can live. It's the reason you were born. It is where synergy and power happen. It's perfect peace and success.

Use the fact that there are no secrets for your good. In Mark 7:24 the Bible says, "Jesus left that place and went to the vicinity of Tyre. He entered a house and did not want anyone to know it; yet he could not keep his presence secret." If you are going to try to have secrets, let them be that you have slipped away to take care of the poor, to pray, to give, to serve. Let others whisper about your secrets: your generosity, your kindness and your caring. Those are the kinds of secrets that we should try to have. Because, for better or worse, others know our secrets. They know and they share. They whisper.

As your dad, I can't tell you how pleased I am to have people whisper about your hard work, your faithfulness to a promise, your love for fine music and your fun-loving, innocent lives. You will keep those attributes all of your life if you will live with the principle in mind that there are no secrets.

I love being your dad,

REFLECTION AND DISCUSSION

1. Is your private life consistent with your public life?
2. Do you have any secrets, or are you living as if there are no secrets?
3. What practical steps can you take to ensure that you are living a life of integrity?
4. If someone confessed a secret to you, what would you tell them?
5. What three things did the old tent preacher say and what do they mean to you? Give an example of each point.
6. What two lies often come to people's minds when they are contemplating doing something wrong? How would you respond to each of these thoughts?
7. Whose decisions determine the quality of your life?

FEAR GOD, NOT PEOPLE

January 30

Dear Christy and Marcus,

You two are incredible! I am on a plane right now, returning from Florida, and I'm thinking about how you have shown so much integrity in your lives lately. Marcus, I really appreciate the tender heart you have for the situations that some of your friends have found themselves in. I loved it when you called me to ask me to find some resources to help your friend's family out of a difficult situation. I think you are a great young man with a huge heart for others.

And Christy, I so appreciate the decisions you have been making about the boys who are interested in developing a closer relationship with you. Your character and wisdom are evident in the way you are kind and courteous, but not enamored by their acceptance and desires to be with you. Good job, Christy! I'm proud of you.

I recently memorized the part of Galatians 1 where Paul writes:

Am I now trying to win the approval of men, or of God? Or am I trying to please men? If I were still trying to please men, I would not be a servant of Christ (v. 10).

With the kinds of decisions you two have been making lately, it's obvious that you are trying to please God and not be controlled by other people's opinions. That is a great strength. Don't ever lose it. Too many people are so wrapped up in concerns for acceptance and in fear of rejection that they are unable to make their decisions independent of the crowd. They're scared of what other people think, which keeps them from having personal integrity.

Jesus spoke about this in Luke 12 when He said,

> I tell you, my friends, do not be afraid of those who kill the body and after that can do no more. But I will show you whom you should fear: Fear him who, after the killing of the body, has power to throw you into hell. Yes, I tell you, fear him. Are not five sparrows sold for two pennies? Yet not one of them is forgotten by God. Indeed, the very hairs of your head are all numbered. Don't be afraid; you are worth more than many sparrows. I tell you, whoever acknowledges me before men, the Son of Man will also acknowledge him before the angels of God. But he who disowns me before men will be disowned before the angels of God. And everyone who speaks a word against the Son of Man will be forgiven, but anyone who blasphemes against the Holy Spirit will not be forgiven (vv. 4-10).

As Jesus makes clear, there is a hell, and it's God who has established the rules about who goes there and who doesn't. I know that sounds old-fashioned, and both of you have teachers and friends who would scowl at you for believing in hell. But whether people accept it or not, the Bible teaches that hell is a real place—a place from which God made a great sacrifice to provide us deliverance. Going through life choosing to dismiss hell as simply a myth is like believing that people who jump out of airplanes without parachutes don't suffer when they hit the ground. If you jump without a parachute, you will suffer regardless of what you believe. If you end this life without God's gift of salvation, you'll also suffer—but for eternity. So, Jesus' words highlight the second key to successful living:

FEAR GOD, NOT PEOPLE.

Yesterday I wrote to you about living as if there are no secrets, and that idea is inherently related to today's letter. Paul stresses them both in 2 Corinthians 5 when he writes,

> For we must all appear before the judgment seat of Christ, that each one may receive what is due him for the things done while in the body, whether good or bad. [See, there are no secrets!] Since, then, we know what it is to fear the Lord, we try to persuade men (vv. 10-11).

I'll never forget the first time I actually realized the meaning of these verses. In 1980 I went to Seoul, South Korea, with Daniel Ost, a great missionary to Mexico. While we were in Seoul, we went to an all-night prayer meeting with over 10,000 people in attendance. When we walked onto the platform at about 1:30 A.M. to speak to those who had gathered to pray, I glanced down at my Bible and saw those verses from 2 Corinthians. Then, in a split second, my eyes were opened into the spiritual world.

I saw terrible human suffering. I saw people trying to find relief from their horrible anguish. They were screaming, clawing, gasping, crawling, moaning, hating and blaming. I was aghast. It was so offensive and appalling that I could hardly breathe. It was the most ghastly, grim, repulsive and disgusting sight I had ever seen. I was shocked at the sheer grief and agony. These people were hopeless, unable to find help. There was no way they could end their own suffering.

I had seen suffering before, but never like this. I'd been among starving people in India. I'd seen people suffering because of drought. I'd witnessed the terrible pain and disorientation in the aftermath of an earthquake. I'd visited hospitals and homes when people died or learned of the death of a loved one. I'd seen parents wincing in agony over children killed in accidents. But none of that compared to this.

I was seeing into hell. I was seeing the terror of the Lord.

I think it was so uniquely horrifying because it had no end. All earthly suffering has an end, but hell goes on forever. In hell, there is no way to stop it. No painkillers; no completion; no way to commit suicide. It just keeps going.

Thank God my glimpse didn't last more than a split second. I couldn't have taken it. And I was only *looking*. I didn't personally experience any suffering. I just saw it. As I regained my composure, I reminded myself that God didn't design hell for people, but because people had chosen to reject God and live for themselves, they had to suffer the punishment for their sin. The people in hell were people who didn't fear God. They scoffed at His attempt to rescue them by not responding to His love.

Shaken, I sat down in the chair on the platform and opened my Bible to John 3 to remind myself of Jesus' words:

> For God did not send his Son into the world to condemn the world, but to save the world through him. Whoever believes in him is not condemned, but whoever does not believe stands condemned already because he has not believed in the name of God's one and only Son (vv. 17-18).

God never intended for people to go to hell. They start on the road there while on Earth, and continue on it into eternity. That's why the story of Jesus is such good news, and why it has the affection of billions of people. Jesus interrupted our path to destruction and gave us the power to change directions.

I know, I know. People will say to you, "If God loves people so much, why should anyone go to hell?"

Paul said that the love of God (see 2 Cor. 5:14) and the terror of the Lord (see 2 Cor. 7:1) were both strong motivators in his life. It's two sides of the same coin. God loves people, and He hates it when people don't fear Him. God loves people, but His awesome holiness demands not only our affection but our obedience and reverence. He loves it when we show a respect for Him that has an element of holy fear.

The writings of David make this abundantly clear. He understood the mysterious connection between the love of God and the fear of God. In Psalm 36, David writes,

> An oracle is within my heart concerning the sinfulness of the wicked: There is no fear of God before his eyes. For in his own eyes he flatters himself too much to detect or hate his sin. The words of his mouth are wicked and deceitful; he has ceased to be wise and to do good. Even on his bed he plots evil; he commits himself to a sinful course and does not reject what is wrong (vv. 1-4).

Then David goes right to the other side of the coin: Love. He writes in the same psalm,

> Your love, O LORD, reaches to the heavens, your faithfulness to the skies. Your righteousness is like the mighty mountains, your justice like the great deep. O LORD, you preserve both man and beast. How priceless is

your unfailing love! Both high and low among men find refuge in the shadow of your wings. They feast on the abundance of your house; you give them drink from your river of delights. For with you is the fountain of life; in your light we see light (vv. 5-9).

People don't talk much anymore about the fear of God; many people have a hard time understanding it. But it's still true, and it's vitally important for us to grasp as we try to be the people God wants us to be. The best example I can think of to help you understand the fear of the Lord is to tell you about my relationship with my dad. He was a wonderful man. He loved me, provided for me, enjoyed spending time with me and was always a person I could be proud of. But I knew that if I was arrogant, selfish or unkind, Dad's wrath would be directed toward me. I feared Dad. I respected Dad. I wanted to please Dad. I loved it when he was laughing, but was well aware that he had the ability to discipline me firmly. This is like the fear of God. God loves us, yes, but He will also discipline us firmly.

After getting my first glimpse of the terror of the Lord on that platform in Seoul, I was deeply shaken. And I want you to be shaken as well. In order to live the kind of life that will be prosperous and powerful, we all have to understand the terror of the Lord. What I saw and read scared me, but then John 3 made sense:

This is the verdict: Light has come into the world, but men loved darkness instead of light because their deeds were evil. Everyone who does evil hates the light, and will not come into the light for fear that his deeds will be exposed (v. 19).

Now I knew that the way to love light is to fear God; it's the best motivation for living as if there are no secrets.

When you were growing up, we would try to motivate you to do the right thing by encouraging you, loving you, training you and educating you. But sometimes, if you wanted to do something wrong that might be dangerous, we would have to threaten you. It's like Moses said in Exodus 20:20: "Do not be afraid. God has come to test you, so that the fear of God will be with you to keep you from sinning." In other words, don't be afraid, because God loves you. But be afraid, because God loves you. Do you understand?

In the end, people who fear God and put their trust in what Christ has done for them on the cross live life well. They are the most successful, most godly people. That's why the Bible stresses over and over again the importance of fearing God. It's foundational to everything we believe:

- When God was testing Abraham's obedience by seeing if he was willing to sacrifice Isaac on the altar, God said to Abraham: "Do not lay a hand on the boy. . . . Do not do anything to him. Now *I know that you fear God*, because you have not withheld from me your son, your only son" (Gen. 22:12, emphasis added).

- Remember Joseph, the young man who resisted Potiphar's wife and was thrown into prison because of her false accusation? Well, Joseph ended up being the second most powerful man in all of Egypt. The Bible makes it clear that one of Joseph's primary characteristics was that he feared God (see Gen. 42:18).

- When Moses was organizing the new nation of Israel, one of the qualifications of a leader was the fear of God. In Exodus, the Bible says: "But select capable men from all the people—men who *fear God*, trustworthy men who hate dishonest gain—and appoint them as officials over thousands, hundreds, fifties and tens" (18:21, emphasis added).

- Uzziah was one of the greatest kings in Judah He came to the throne when he was 16 years old, and reigned successfully for 52 years. God was pleased with him, and so were his people. Obviously, though, he had decided to be a strong man early in his life. Second Chronicles says, "[King Uzziah] sought God during the days of Zechariah, who instructed him in the *fear of God*. As long as he sought the LORD, God gave him success" (26:5, emphasis added).

- Solomon, one of the wisest men of all time, wrote that the number one way to improve our quality of life is to fear the Lord. In Ecclesiastes, Solomon writes: "Although a wicked man commits a hundred crimes and still lives a long time, I know that it will go better with *God-fearing* men, who are reverent before God. Yet because the wicked do not fear God, it will not go well with them, and their days will not lengthen like a shadow" (8:12-13, emphasis added).

- When Jesus was being crucified, one of the thieves cynically said to Him, "Aren't you the Christ? Save yourself and us!" The Bible records that the other thief rebuked him by saying, "Don't you *fear God* . . . since you are under the same sentence? We are punished justly, for we are getting what our deeds deserve. But this man has done nothing wrong." Then he continued by wisely saying, "Jesus, remember me when you come into your kingdom." To this, Jesus responded, "I tell you the truth, today you will be with me in paradise" (see Luke 23:39-43, emphasis added). Here, the fear of God distinguished between the one who knew who Jesus was and the one who was cynical. Their eternal destinies hung in the balance of whether or not they feared God.

• Finally, John records in Revelation, the last book of the Bible, that the angel who comes to proclaim the gospel to every nation on Earth shouts: "*Fear God* and give him glory, because the hour of his judgment has come. Worship him who made the heavens, the earth, the sea and the springs of water" (14:7, emphasis added).

There we have it. From Genesis to Revelation, in the lives of some of the most influential people in biblical history, the Bible is saying: "Fear God!" It's foundational to our very existence. Solomon even went so far as to say that the whole duty of man is to "fear God and keep his commandments" (Eccles. 12:13).

When I was in my early 20s, I took several hundred high school students to Hattiesburg, Mississippi, for a weeklong summer camp. One afternoon everyone was playing baseball, and I was standing on the sidelines enjoying watching the game.

While watching, the Holy Spirit came upon me and said, "If you will obey me, your life will work like this." I continued to watch the game in amazement: All of a sudden, the team that was up to bat started hitting every ball pitched to them, while the opposing team couldn't catch, make accurate throws or make good decisions. The team up to bat scored again and again. It was incredible.

I watched and laughed as some of the best athletes made fools out of themselves, while mediocre players were playing as if they were in the major leagues. I was amazed at the power of God.

After several minutes of this, the Holy Spirit came on me again and said, "If you disobey me, your life will go like this." Instantly the dynamic on the field changed. The team up to bat still got a few hits, but they had to work hard for them. They still ran a few bases, but every base was a struggle. The opposition became formidable. Even though there were still advances, it was hard work. Every victory had to be earned. Nothing was given.

I don't know if it works this way in everyone's life, but I do know that this experience helped me to love and fear God. I realized the greatness and graciousness of God. He wants to use all of us, and we can best be used if we determine in our hearts to live in His grace and power and not to step outside His will through disobedience. He tries to encourage us with His love and mercy, and it is His kindness that sustains us. But He also disciplines those He loves, just as a good father disciplines his children.

Christy and Marcus, it's important that we all know the grace, love and forgiveness of God. But it's equally important that we fear, honor and respect Him, knowing that He is holy and that He is dedicated to working His life into us.

When we came here to Colorado Springs, we had nothing. In January of 1985, we started the church with a handful of people in the basement of our home, and now God has given us a wonderful church of over 8,000 people who love God and enjoy serving Him with us. By all accounts, it looks as if God's best plan all along had been for us to serve Him here.

But there's something about the story of Colorado Springs that I very seldom share with people: I don't think I was God's first choice to minister to the people of this city.

When we first moved to Colorado Springs, the Lord showed me that there were three other men He had chosen for this city before me, but all of them had failed in one way or another. They were all fine people, but had gotten off track or been misled somehow. God told me that I was His fourth choice for Colorado Springs, not His first, and that I needed to walk in obedience to Him.

Then He showed me another brother whom He had also brought to Colorado Springs. This other brother was a better speaker than I, a stronger student of the Bible and had a more disciplined prayer life. But people were not responding to his preaching; they were responding to mine.

As I prayed, the Lord showed me that if I disobeyed Him, people would simply stop responding to my preaching. I understood then that *God* builds His Church and that *God* opens the hearts people to respond to the gospel. This realization caused me to both love and fear God. If I disobeyed, He would ensure that my speaking would not move their hearts and He would cause people to start responding to the other man's speaking. I was scared, but very interested, because I had seen the hard work and the struggles of the previous three men who were chosen for Colorado Springs. I realized then that God could use anyone He wanted to, but rewarded obedience. If I would obey, He would institute His sovereign plan. So I was highly motivated to cooperate!

I told God that I couldn't stand the pressure and that I wanted Him to establish a time when I would know that I had either failed the test or passed the test. He told me I would know that I had failed the test if this other brother started drawing crowds and New Life started losing its spiritual authority. But if I passed the test, I would know by the other brother being called elsewhere. He said, "If you pass the test, I will call him to another city and give him a significant ministry to reward him for his faithfulness in obeying me in Colorado Springs, even though I never gave him fruit here."

I can't tell you how relieved I was one morning at breakfast when this brother told me he was moving to another city. He said that God told him, "You have been faithful to me, and I am calling you to another city to reward you for your obedience to me in Colorado Springs." He asked me if I thought such a strange message could be from God. I smiled and told him that I thought he was hearing God's voice clearly and that God would indeed richly reward him. Now he's pastoring a major church in another city and will have heard "the rest of the story" if he reads these letters I'm writing to you.

You see, Christy and Marcus, I don't think my primary calling in life is to be a pastor. I believe that I am a missionary, called to reach unreached people groups or the least evangelized people. Before God called me to Colorado Springs, I was thinking about some of the super megacities of the world and wondering how to move all of us there to serve the most needy people on Earth. Then God instructed me to come to Colorado Springs to build New Life Church, Praise Mountain and the World Prayer Center. I was shocked and a little embarrassed when God called me to Colorado Springs, because I had preached so hard and so long on the need to go to the unreached nations. But God selected me to come to Colorado Springs so I could use the resources here to reach people there. Today, we're doing more for world missions from Colorado Springs than we ever could have done directly from the field. How is it possible? Because God is great. God is good. God must be obeyed. He is trustworthy and faithful to all of us if we love Him and fear Him.

Let me show you one more set of verses on this idea. In Malachi, the Bible says:

> "So I will come near to you for judgment. I will be quick to testify against sorcerers, adulterers and perjurers, against those who defraud laborers of their wages, who oppress the widows and the fatherless, and deprive aliens of justice, but do not fear me," says the LORD Almighty (3:5).

Christy and Marcus, it's good to have God as your friend and not as your enemy. If you fear God and serve him, you won't become a sorcerer, adulterer or perjurer. The fear of God will cause you to be fair and just and to provide for those in need.

Look how Malachi's prophesy ends:

> Then those who feared the LORD talked with each other, and the LORD listened and heard. A scroll of remembrance was written in his presence concerning those who feared the LORD and honored his name. "They will be mine," says the LORD Almighty, "in the day when I make up my treasured possession. I will spare them, just as in compassion a man spares his son who serves him. And you will again see the distinction between the righteous and the wicked, between those who serve God and those who do not" (vv. 16-18).

Live as if there are no secrets, and the scroll of remembrance will speak in your favor. Fear God, and you will be distinguished with the righteous. Don't forget: You are one of His treasured possessions (which is what I'm writing you about next!).

I believe the fear of God is a gift. Christy and Marcus, please contemplate this letter. Pray for the fear of God. Choose to fear God. Receive the fear of God.

I love being your dad,

Dad

REFLECTION AND DISCUSSION

1. What do you think Paul means when he says, "Since, then, we know what it is to fear the Lord, we try to persuade men. What we are is plain to God, and I hope it is also plain to your conscience" (2 Cor. 5:11)? What did it mean to Paul to fear the Lord?

2. How are the fear of God and the love of God two sides of the same coin?

3. Can you think of a time when the fear of God kept you from doing something you shouldn't do?

4. Why is it important to direct your fear away from people and toward God? What does it say about us when we are scared of what people think?

5. Give an example of a time when fear of a person in authority motivated you to do the right thing.

6. Give an example of a person doing the wrong thing because they had no fear of God.

REALIZE HOW MUCH GOD VALUES YOU

February 6

Dear Christy and Marcus,

Reading the paper this morning was an unsettling experience. Page after page was filled with stories of people making horrible mistakes. In the last few days alone, police uncovered a plot to burn down a local elementary school; a 66-year-old man shot four people in a factory; and, for the second time in two weeks, a group of high school kids was discovered making pipe bombs to blow up their school.

Whew! What are they thinking? People seem to be feeling more unstable and vulnerable than ever before. Millions of people are in trouble. Millions of people are in need.

And I believe that is why God needs people like you.

I am so convinced that God has chosen you and wants to use you. Without a doubt, God is doing wonderful things in you as you seek Him. That's why I'm so enjoying reading Luke 12 and writing to you about these principles. I want you to live the very best life, the life God desires for you.

I hope that the letter about fearing God stimulated some good thinking for both of you. One of the problems that people sometimes have when they learn about the fear of God is that they don't understand how God feels about them. They hear a pastor say, "Fear God!" and in their minds they automatically add, "Because He is out to get you, you little worm!"

But in Luke 12, after Jesus emphasizes that there are no secrets and then explains the importance of fearing God, He introduces an idea that gives context to His teaching:

> Are not five sparrows sold for two pennies? Yet not one of them is forgotten by God. Indeed, the very hairs of your head are all numbered. Don't be afraid; you are worth more than many sparrows (vv. 6-7).

Jesus is saying it clearly: God is big and worthy to be feared, but He loves you. You are valuable to Him. And this highlights the third principle for successful living that I want to share with you:

REALIZE HOW MUCH GOD VALUES YOU!

As you go to school and read the papers, you'll find that some of our scholars are teaching the wrong ideas about what it means to be human. They say that we are no different from animals; that we are biological accidents produced through millions of years of evolution. They say we have no more or less intrinsic value than cows, chickens and pigs. They believe we are scientific oddities—just species that have appeared on Earth for a short while and will eventually die out.

That might be true if there were no God, but there is! He stands over His creation with loving care. He made human beings for specific purposes. You are valuable to Him. He created you with a specific purpose and plan in mind. And He likes you so much that the plan He has for you is a good one.

I'll never forget when I first learned this lesson. As I was praying one day several years ago, God began to remind me of Scriptures that use the word "grace." I grabbed my Bible and looked up every instance of the word I could find in the New Testament. As I read, I was shocked to discover that the Church's popular definition of grace was not entirely accurate. All my life, I'd heard that "grace" meant "unmerited favor." But as I studied, I learned that the word "grace" actually meant simply "favor."

Certainly it's true that God's grace is unmerited—we don't deserve it—but the way some emphasize this theological truth subverts the benevolent tone of the meaning of the word "grace." Too often the Church has told people that although they can be saved because of Jesus' sacrifice, they are essentially worthless and disliked by God. It's true that if people choose to live their own lives void of God's plan—if they reject God—they end just as Scripture warns: a vapor, a breath, a blade of grass that will quickly dry up and blow away; here today, gone tomorrow, often not to be remembered two generations later. But some teachers wrongly, and maybe unintentionally, communicate that God doesn't want to save us in the first place, that He despises us and can hardly stand us because we are so terrible, but He will because he has to. So we're saved—barely.

Don't believe that. It's just not true. Jesus died willingly. A reluctant savior He is not. He loves you too much to hesitate at all. God chose you for Himself before the creation of the world (see Eph. 1:4). He knew you before you were born (see Ps. 139:13-15), and now He has revealed Himself to you by His Spirit because He wants to. You are valuable to God.

Of course, the devil would love for you to fail. But I won't let him. I'm here to help you succeed. Why? Because, like God, I want to. Did you earn it? No, but that doesn't matter. It's not the point.

The point is that I want the best for you. I love you. I learned it from God. It's the way He is toward all His children.

God gave His grace for us because He wanted to. He accepts you. He wants to bless you. He wants to benefit you. He loves giving you gifts and working His joy into your life. God has many blessings to give, and He wants to give them to you liberally. He takes pleasure in pouring Himself into you. He thinks you are worth all the effort. He doesn't resist you at all. He loves it when you seek Him so He can respond to you. He loves you, and He likes you, too. Very much.

God's grace is His favor, His blessing, His gifts and His nature freely given. It's His influence on your heart reflected in your life. It's the power of God to take everything negative and sinful out of your life and fill you with His life. It's His way of saying, "I love you!"

That's why Paul begins so many of his letters by saying, "Grace and peace to you" (see Rom. 1:7; 1 Cor. 1:3; 2 Cor. 1:2; Gal. 1:3; Eph. 1:2; Phil. 1:2; Col. 1:2; 1 Thess. 1:1, 2 Thess. 1:2). He changed it to "Grace, mercy and peace from God the Father and Christ Jesus our Lord" in his letters to young Timothy (see 1 Tim. 1:2 and 2 Tim. 1:2), and to "Grace to you and peace from God our Father and the Lord Jesus Christ" when he wrote to his friend Philemon (see Philem. 1:3). The word "grace" is used 93 times in the *New International Version* of the New Testament. Why such an emphasis? Because God wants people to know about His favor toward them.

Remember when the angel was announcing the coming of the Lord Jesus? He said, "Glory to God in the highest, and on earth peace to men *on whom his favor rests*" (Luke 2:14, emphasis added). This is the core message of Jesus' life. Since He died on the cross, God's favor is available to any person who will respond to it.

So some chemistry teacher might say, "Nice dream, but not true. You are the result of a biological mix of your mom and dad and are worth about 65 cents of carbon. That's what you are."

Don't believe it. You can tell the value of a thing by its purchase price. How much did God pay for you? Sixty-five cents? A dollar? A million dollars? A continent? A solar system? A galaxy? God wanted you so much that He gave His one and only Son as a purchase price for you. He paid with the death of His most precious Son for you. That's your worth. You are so valuable to God that He was willing to pay everything He had for you.

When people throw their lives away through alcohol, drugs, immorality or other kinds of foolish living, it is obvious that they don't know or can't believe that God has a better plan for their lives. Because they live as if there is such a thing as a secret, and they have no fear of God, their lives are often wasted. They don't maximize their value. They become just a breath—here today and gone tomorrow—because they never discover the reason that God created them.

I don't want that to be the case with the two of you. I want you to find your finest purpose. God knew the circumstances of your birth and design and the purpose for your life before your mom and I ever met. He loves you and designed you to accomplish a task. Everything about you can be used to contribute to that task, or you can, like so many others, squander your uniqueness and miss God's reason for creating you.

You have no obligation to waste your life. You don't have to be immoral, greedy, angry or selfish. You don't have to spend your life on materialism, selfishness, hatred or sensuality. You can resist sin, live for God, pray and fast and let His confidence grow in you as you find your special worth and value in Him. God wants you to be okay. God wants you to live by His Word and plan.

Christy and Marcus, in order to live well, you will have to trust that your Designer created you the way you are for a reason. Very often people miss God's plan for their lives because they don't know that God gave them certain appearances, abilities, families and surroundings for a good reason. If they evaluate these areas according to other people's standards, they sometimes become unhappy about themselves. They're prevented from using what they have been given to improve the lives of others. If, on the other hand, they understand that God has given them a unique set of gifts that they can use for His glory, they can receive power from God to improve every area of their lives.

So many people blow their lives right here. They are either so self-centered that they become the type of people others can't stand to be around, or they go the other way and are so timid and fearful that they make everyone miserable. Thinking more highly of yourself than you ought is repugnant, and becoming an overly timid weasel is equally repulsive. The right way to think of yourself is the way God thinks of you: You are valuable and here for a purpose.

So accept the fact that God thinks you are valuable, without using that information to rain accolades on yourself. Instead, use it to serve others confidently.

I know you realize that's a little trickier than it sounds. How do we think of ourselves just the right away? How do we know if we're balanced—not too self-absorbed and not too timid and fearful? Years ago, I developed a little checklist I use to make sure I strike the balance. If you use this same list, I'm sure it will serve you through the years as it has served me.

1. *Use wisdom in the way you dress.*
Remember the two boys who ended up killing the kids at Columbine High School? They were known around campus because their choice of clothing called attention to themselves. When people have internal issues that are not resolved, they often reflect their confusion in the way they dress. As you go through the years, honorably reflect your gender and stylishly represent your age. You know how terrible it is when a teenage

girl is a little overanxious to display her new figure, or when a teenage boy wears his pants too tight, or when a 60-year-old dresses like a 21-year-old. Ugh! It's just not right.

Dress modestly and stylishly. Be sensitive to tendencies to give too much attention to clothing or to develop a lazy attitude that says that clothes don't matter. First Timothy 2:9 says to "dress modestly, with decency and propriety." These are simple instructions (that can apply to both sexes, though Paul is addressing women). Wear clothes that communicate that you are a respectable, moral person who understands etiquette. If clothes are an issue, there is probably an unresolved internal issue. Settle the internal issues and wear reasonable clothes.

2. *Trust God with the details of your appearance and your heritage.*
Regularly I talk to people who are unhappy with their bodies. Other people complain miserably about the family they come from, the neighborhood they were raised in or some misfortune they have had to face. Still others are convinced that it's easier for everyone else than it is for them. Most of these people are worried about things that they can't do much about, and they would be better off by trusting God with those details.

David said,

I praise you because I am fearfully and wonderfully made; your works are wonderful, I know that full well. My frame was not hidden from you when I was made in the secret place. When I was woven together in the depths of the earth, your eyes saw my unformed body. All the days ordained for me were written in your book before one of them came to be (Ps. 139:14-16).

This is an incredible set of verses. Look closely at them. God puts us together in detail. He knows the color of our hair, the shape of our body. He gave them to us for a reason. If we'll stop whining and start thanking God for the way He made us, it will do something incredible to the way we view life. Paul says that we are "God's workmanship, created in Christ Jesus to do good works, which God prepared in advance for us to do" (Eph. 2:10). We should thank God for our bodies, our families, our heritage and the details of our lives. For the things that we can change, we should take responsibility to make ourselves better prepared for the calling God has on our lives. For the things we can't change, we need to use them as best we can for the benefit of the kingdom of God. But in it all, we have to remember that we belong to God. He can use any difficulty we face to develop inner character qualities and to serve others if we make the core decision to trust Him with everything. This kind of trust and surrender brings us contentment. And contentment is a powerful tool for building a foundation for successful living.

3.   *Have confidence in relationships with others.*

If people struggle with their appearance or their ability to trust God, they can either become so aggressive that they are objectionable or so shy that they become reclusive. We all need the strength of conviction that God is good and that He created us to be strong enough to serve, humble enough to lead and kind enough to listen. Maintaining the right balance between arrogance and timidity is a great skill to be mastered, and it can be mastered as you relate positively to God's design of you. Christy and Marcus, you were created for the purpose of being His hand in the lives of others to influence them toward Him or toward things that improve their lives.

4.   *Love others.*

A simple definition for love is "to live for someone else's good." In other words, when you say to someone that you love them, you are saying that you are willing to do what needs to be done for their lives to go well. If someone tells you that they love you, if they are mature, they are saying that they will do what's best for you, not for them.

Most people think that love is an emotion. Very often, love is accompanied by emotion, but the emotion will come and go. People who live according to emotional love have unstable, rocky relationships at best. But people who are able to make quality decisions about who and what they will love are strong and stable.

First Corinthians 13 says:

Love is patient, love is kind. It does not envy, it does not boast, it is not proud. It is not rude, it is not self-seeking, it is not easily angered, it keeps no record of wrongs (vv. 4-5).

This thought is completed by saying:

[Love] always protects, always trusts, always hopes, always perseveres. Love never fails (vv. 7-8).

When Jesus was asked to identify the greatest command-ments in the Scriptures, He responded,

"Love the Lord your God with all your heart and with all your soul and with all your mind and with all your strength." The second is this: "Love your neighbor as yourself." There is no commandment greater than these (Mark 12:30-31).

If love is a commandment, then it is also a decision. Love is not a feeling floating through the air that will strike you sometimes. No—you can make decisions about who and what you will love, and who and what you won't love. One of the greatest things any person can do is make a strong decision early in life that they will love themselves and others as creations of God, and to reserve a special, unique love for family members, spouses, lifelong friendships and others God has placed in their lives.

The word "love" is used 232 times in the *New International Version* of the New Testament. It would be wise for you to take a few evenings and look up "love" throughout the New Testament and learn the great joy that can be found in true love.

5. *Accept yourself.*

In order to love others, you have to have enough confidence in God to love yourself. Too often people are consumed in excessive self-criticism, which usually means they are consumed in self-centeredness. They need to accept themselves and get on with the work of making the world a better place.

Isaiah 45:9-10 says:

Woe to him who quarrels with his Maker, to him who is but a potsherd among the potsherds on the ground. Does the clay say to the potter, "What are you making?" Does your work say, "He has no hands"? Woe to him who says to his father, "What have you begotten?" or to his mother, "What have you brought to birth?"

As believers, our role is to be grateful to God for creating us and to take care of ourselves so we can serve Him. The road of self-criticism is endless and treacherous. Rather than whining and complaining about the way He made us, we need to get over ourselves. Life is not about us—it's about others.

6. *Relax and enjoy life.*

Several years ago I went water-skiing with a rather large and serious pastor from the United Methodist Church. For most of the day, he just sat still in the boat and watched. Whenever I sat near him, he'd strike up some conversation that was far too serious for the mood of the afternoon. After a while, I was able to talk him into getting onto a raft behind the boat, so I could pull him. He lay on the raft and held tightly onto the ski rope. I gave the boat the full throttle, but because the pastor was so heavy, the boat wouldn't pull him out of the water. Instead, he dragged in the water with the raft rippling down his backside and a wave of spray coming over him. All I could see from the boat was the spray flying all around him, but I could hear him laughing loud and hard. The spray was tickling his belly!

At that moment, God spoke to me: "I'm enjoying this pastor more right now than I have in years."

God likes to enjoy people and He likes to laugh. He loves it when people enjoy Him. After this experience, I decided that when God looks at all the hatred, betrayal, sorrow and grief in the earth, and then His eyes get to me, I want Him to smile. I want to make God enjoy me. And I want God to enjoy you, too. Live lives that please Him, and you'll have a great life.

7. *Be humble.*

Proverbs 11:2 says: "When pride comes, then comes disgrace, but with humility comes wisdom." People who allow pride to come into their hearts are headed for trouble. You've both seen this principle at work over and over again. Remember all the fairy tales you heard growing up about the proud king or prince who was headed for a downfall? And have you noticed that the kids at school who are too cool for everyone else end up making fools of themselves at one time or another? That's a biblical principle at work: "Pride goes before destruction, a haughty spirit before a fall" (Prov. 16:18).

Christy and Marcus, remember that the thing that makes Jesus different from all the other "gods" is that He *humbled* Himself. The Creator allowed Himself to be crucified. This is what makes Him so wonderful, and this is what makes Him so powerful. He chose to be humble because it served a better, higher purpose. In the same way, we must choose to be humble even when we think we deserve honor. We need to keep deflecting praise away from ourselves, and toward God. He deserves it, and He will bless us for protecting His worship.

8.   *Keep your priorities in order.*
Sometimes people fall into traps because they let their priorities get mixed up. They know that family is important, but they spend more time with friends. They know that seeking God is important, but they let themselves become totally consumed with work. This is usually alright for a while, but sooner or later it can lead to big trouble.

The secret here is to know your purpose in life. What does God want you to do? Why were you created? If you understand your fundamental purpose, then it's simple to keep your priorities straight—just make sure you are doing the things that will fulfill that purpose. I know my purpose in life is to be a senior pastor for a local church, so I spend the vast majority of my time building and strengthening our church. I also like scuba diving, and sometimes it sounds like a lot more fun to go scuba diving than it does to outline a sermon. But pastoring is my purpose, so it is my priority.

Don't ever start believing that something is more important than it really is. Keep things in their proper place. Clothes are just clothes, cars just cars, jobs just jobs. The most important thing in life is to love and serve God and to love and serve people.

Christy and Marcus, as you read and reread this letter, please don't make the mistake of thinking that I'm saying that God values you just because I'm your dad. I do love you a great deal, but these ideas are straight from God Himself. Meditate on the Scriptures I've listed or quoted above. Realize how much God values you. He has an amazing plan for your life, and He loves it when you respond to Him.

I love you, and I love being your dad,

REFLECTION AND DISCUSSION

1. In what way does God need people?
2. What's the difference between "favor" and "unmerited favor"?
3. How are you doing on the checklist?
4. What does knowing your purpose in life have to do with your perspective on yourself?

ACKNOWLEDGE GOD IN A PAGAN CULTURE

February 10

Dear Christy and Marcus,

I heard the gospel for the first time shortly after my sophomore year of high school. I went to a big Campus Crusade for Christ meeting with a group of my friends, listened to Bill Bright explain the gospel and gave my life to Christ. Right away, I was radically changed.

During my sophomore year, I had been popular at school but was not always a positive influence on my friends. When I became a Christian, I was concerned about the effect it would have on my friendships. I hated the thought that some of them might reject my new faith or resent the change in my life. So I decided to bring as many of them along with me as I could.

One of the first things I did was buy a Christian symbol I could wear around my neck. I wore it all the time. It was like nothing anyone at my school had ever seen—it was a fish symbol with a Greek word whose letters ("Ichthus") inside the fish stand for "Jesus Christ, God-Son-Savior." I know you've seen that symbol on cars or T-shirts, but I don't think I've ever told you its history before. In the early years of Christianity, believers were under intense persecution from the Roman state. Christians had to be very secretive about their faith. So, if you were a believer and you saw someone else you thought might be a Christian, you would go near them and draw a curved line in the sand. If they were a Christian, they would get the signal and draw another curved line connected to yours—thereby completing the "fish."

Anyway, I found a little bronze version of this symbol and tied it around my neck with a leather string. It looked really great—very first century. I wish I still had it to show you.

Since this thing around my neck looked so cool and was so unusual, the symbol started to become popular around school. Before long, it was trendy to have a necklace with this Christian symbol. And, since it had strange Greek letters on it, people would regularly ask me what it meant, and I would explain the meaning of the letters and the fish symbol.

That same year, there was a teen ministry trying to work with students in our school, but they were having a tough time drawing a crowd. When they heard about my conversion, they contacted me about coming to their meeting. I didn't like the setting or the style of the meeting, so I offered to host the meeting at my house. Kids from school were used to coming to my house for parties, so it was natural for them to come over. We started, and the place was immediately jam-packed. Lots of my friends gave their lives to Christ through those meetings.

At the same time, we started offering youth activities at the church I was attending. Our groups spilled over and became a major hub of activity in our school. I'm sure that some kids or adults were nervous about it, but since I was the one driving it, there wasn't much they could say. I was just one of the high school guys. I wasn't being coached by any outside group. I'd just made a decision to read a chapter of my Bible every night before I went to bed and to bring as many of my friends into relationship with God as I could.

Last summer I found my old journal from my high school days. In it I talked about targeting kids with prayer and witnessing. I wrote in my journal about how my friends and I designed strategies to get certain friends into our meeting or on a campout or bike trip (we used to ride all over the state during the summer for fun). Since we were the "cool, outgoing ones," we had a great deal of success with other students. And because of this, a large number of students from my high school class are in full-time ministry today or are strong Christian business leaders. It made high school lots of fun. It gave it purpose. It gave it drive. It was exciting.

I know this might sound like I became a crusader for the gospel while in high school. Maybe I did. But it didn't feel like it at the time. I was the managing editor of our high school newspaper, played several sports, and was both a class officer and involved in leading several of the other clubs in school. I was always busy on weekends and dated the most beautiful girls. High school was great for me, and I think it was great because I was highly involved with the life of the school, and I was a Christian. But I wasn't the type of Christian that scared people. I respected people, I honored their view, but wasn't afraid to share mine.

In my last letter, I talked about how the first way Jesus balanced His teaching about the fear of God was to explain how God values people. Well, right after that discussion in Luke 12, Jesus says something else that relates to fearing God instead of people, and it has to do with how we should act out our faith in public. He says,

I tell you, whoever acknowledges me before men, the Son of Man will also acknowledge him before the angels of God. But he who disowns me before men will be disowned before the angels of God (Luke 12:8-9).

Jesus understood two things: God's nature and people's nature. And He wasn't ashamed of either. The Bible says, "Jesus grew in wisdom and stature, and in favor with God and men" (Luke 2:52). This reveals how we should all be—we should all grow in favor with God and men. But some people become so spiritual that they don't know how to relate to the world. Others become so worldly that they miss the power they could have through spiritual life. Jesus found a perfect combination of both. This, then, is the fourth key to successful living that I want to share with you:

ACKNOWLEDGE GOD IN A PAGAN CULTURE.

The Bible records Jesus praying about this in John 17. He says,

My prayer is not that you take them out of the world but that you protect them from the evil one. They are not of the world, even as I am not of it. Sanctify them by the truth; your word is truth. As you sent me into the world, I have sent them into the world (vv. 15-18).

We all believe that God sent Jesus into the world to accomplish a very specific task. Here Jesus is saying that God sent you with a specific purpose as well. He wants you to accomplish something. But to do it, you have to do what Jesus did—discover that mysterious balance between relating well to people and being consumed in God. I think Jesus did both and I think you can too.

So how do we acknowledge God before men? There are very specific ways for us to do it, the first of which is through our actions. The old maxim is true: Actions speak louder than words. If our actions conflict with what we say, then what we say is silenced. Our actions have to prove our love for God.

Several years ago we had a friend who seemed to love his wife and his kids. They attended church together and were involved in school and other community events. One day I received a message that he had become involved with a woman at work who was "a fine Christian woman." Apparently, he felt as though he had found the woman he really should have married, so he left his wife and kids and moved in with this other woman.

I called him and asked him about it. He said that both of them were good Christians and that they were living a happy life together. I asked him about his vow before God to his wife and his moral responsibility for his children. He assured me that they were all okay and that I didn't need to be worried about them.

The next day I drove to the home where he lived with this new woman and waited for him to get home from work. When he pulled up and saw me, he was obviously shocked but was courteous. He invited me into the house, and we sat and talked for a while. After a little bit, I asked him about his new living arrangement. He explained again what a good Christian woman he was living with and how they had found a new church and were looking forward to a happy life together.

I thought about this a moment and then looked him in the eye. "Okay," I said, "I want you to deny Christ to me."

His jaw dropped. "What?" he exclaimed. "I would never do that!"

I repeated my request, and he repeated his refusal. Then I said, "But you already have. You have denied Christ with your actions. You have violated the Scriptures, the lordship of Christ, your marriage vows and your honor in front of your children and the community. I'm not asking you to do anything other than what you have already done. I just think it would be good for you to hear yourself acknowledge it. You *have* denied Christ. You have rejected Him and declared His lack of lordship in your life. So just say it."

He couldn't believe what I was saying. He insisted that he had not denied Christ. I pointed out that Hebrews 6 says that those who have faithfully followed Christ should continue to do so. If they willfully disobey God they are "crucifying the Son of God all over again and subjecting him to public disgrace" (Heb. 6:6).

I explained that he was subjecting Christ to public disgrace at work, with his wife and children, in the community and to everyone he had ever spoken to about Christ. I told him that even non-Christians have standards about wives and children that are higher than his. By his continued insistence to be a Christian, he was mocking the power of Christ. I said that he would do better to admit that Christ is not Lord of his life than to say that Jesus is Lord while denying it with his actions.

He said that I was misreading his life. We were obviously at the end of our conversation, so I left.

Two weeks later I saw him at church with his wife and kids. He told me that he had never dreamed that you could disown Christ with your life, but it had finally dawned on him. He said that he had appreciated our talk about the way we communicate with our lives. To this day I see this couple regularly, recovered and happily married.

Christy and Marcus, we can acknowledge Christ through everything we do. This is why we are so determined to be responsible about movies we watch, places we go, how we drive, how we dress and how we relate to others. We're not timid or afraid—we just want to communicate Christ in our daily lives, from the way we buy and sell property to the way we entertain ourselves.

About a year ago I spoke on spiritual warfare. After the talk a strong, handsome young man came up to me and said that he really appreciated the talk because he liked to watch pornography and was concerned about the spiritual darkness associated with such activity. But after hearing my talk about how to pray and break the powers of darkness, he understood that he could watch pornography and pray afterward and cancel the negative effects of the movies on his spiritual life.

This man was wrong. His prayers would not have worked. God would not have responded to him. Why? Because his actions indicated the true sinfulness of his life, and he couldn't overcome his actions with simple words. How could he pray and get relief in his life? By praying with his feet! The best way for him to pray would have been to not go anywhere near pornography. By praying with his actions, he could communicate love and faithfulness toward God and find great spiritual and emotional freedom.

Once, when the religious authorities were questioning Jesus, He told a story to show them how their actions contrasted with their words. In Matthew 21 Jesus explained,

There was a man who had two sons. He went to the first and said, "Son, go and work today in the vineyard." "I will not," he answered, but later he changed his mind and went. Then the father went to the other son and said the same thing. He answered, "I will, sir," but he did not go. Which of the two did what his father wanted? "The first," they answered. Jesus said to them, "I tell you the truth, the tax collectors and the prostitutes are entering the kingdom of God ahead of you. For John came to you to show you the way of righteousness, and you did not believe him, but the tax collectors and the prostitutes did. And even after you saw this, you did not repent and believe him" (vv. 28-32).

Why was Jesus being so rough? Because He was dealing with the chief priests and the elders of the people who were known for saying one thing and doing another. The common sinners heard the truth and responded with integrity, but these religious people missed the point completely—they appeared to be godly but were really snakes.

Christy and Marcus, I don't want you to fall into this trap. It's a terrible hole to dig out of. Do what the Bible says. Live as if there are no secrets, fear God and not people, realize how much God values you, and honorably and wisely communicate the life of God to those around you. Do it first through your actions, then complement your actions with words.

Not only do we communicate to others with our actions, but we communicate to God as well. By going to places that please Him we are, in a sense, communicating our love, appreciation and devotion to Him. *Our actions are prayers.* And, on the other side of the coin, we can disown Him by going someplace or doing something that would obviously grieve Him. When we intentionally go somewhere that we know wouldn't please Him, we are telling Him that we don't care about Him or His plan for us.

I don't want to make it sound as if acknowledging God is as easy as making the right choices. We do need to make good choices, but in order to do so, we will have to face resistance. At times, it'll be tempting to just go along with the crowd. To truly and honorably acknowledge God with our words and actions, we need courage.

When I was younger, atheism was popular in communist countries. Atheists can be very hostile toward religion, and communist countries would persecute people who believed in God. Because of that persecution, millions of people suffered unnecessarily because the government was intent on promoting atheism.

It was during that time that I realized the importance of Christian radio, television, books and magazines. These tools for expressing faith are very important to believers and to God. Christian T-shirts, bumper stickers, symbols and architecture are ways Christians can acknowledge God before people. Great musical compositions and other forms of art to the glory of God acknowledge Him as well. Tonight, as I'm up late writing this letter to you, I know that God is pleased because this letter is one way of acknowledging the truth of God in our world.

I would rather die than disown Jesus. I don't want to do anything that would dishonor His name, and I don't want to say anything that would disown Him. He's too good.

But I know this position might cost me my life. I hope that the two of you will take the same position. It just takes courage. When you determine to believe something you must accept the fact that there will be others who hate what you believe. It takes determination to be willing to stand alone, to separate from the crowd, to believe something honorable and noble. It takes strength to know that Jesus is Lord and then demonstrate that knowledge in what you do and say.

That's why Paul wrote in 1 Corinthians: "Be on your guard; stand firm in the faith; be men of courage; be strong. Do everything in love" (16:13-14). When Jesus appeared to Paul when he was in trouble before the Sanhedrin, He said, "Take courage! As you have testified about me in Jerusalem, so you must also testify in Rome" (Acts 23:11). Hebrews says: "But Christ is faithful as a son over God's house. And we are his house, if we hold on to our courage and the hope of which we boast" (3:6).

The importance of courage in the believer's life caught my attention like never before when I was reading through the book of Revelation not too long ago. Revelation 21 makes a list of types of people who will be lost forever, and the first group it mentions is the cowardly. It says:

> But the *cowardly*, the unbelieving, the vile, the murderers, the sexually immoral, those who practice magic arts, the idolaters and all liars—their place will be in the fiery lake of burning sulfur. This is the second death (v. 8, emphasis added).

I was shocked when I read this closely. I always knew that the unbelieving would not have salvation, but here the unbelieving is listed as the second group. The first group is the cowards.

Why is this so? Because cowards can't stick with their convictions. They go with the crowd. They can't stand on their own. They are fearful of people rather than God. They don't have backbone. They lack integrity. This is the only place in the *New International Version* of the New Testament that this word is found, and it is close to the back of the book. It's one of God's final comments. I think it's worth noting.

Let me add one more fundamental idea to this letter before I go to bed. As your dad I understand that it is a lot easier to be in comfort, peace and abundance than it is to suffer. And I understand that right now in our lives we have plenty of food, we're able to work and earn what we need and want, and we are able to travel and work in safety and peace. No doubt about it—things are great.

But most of the world doesn't live this way. As we grow, we should understand that our personal comfort is not the highest ideal in life. We need to believe with conviction; no matter what our circumstances in life are. If godliness opens the door for us to prosper and have an abundance of things, we are grateful. But if godliness leads us to prison, suffering or maybe even death, then we must be grateful still. The issue here is godliness, not what we can get out of it.

Jesus is, of course, the perfect example of this. In Luke 24 Jesus says:

> The Christ will suffer and rise from the dead on the third day, and repentance and forgiveness of sins will be preached in his name to all nations, beginning at Jerusalem (vv. 46-47).

Because Jesus was willing to suffer, we have forgiveness of sins and relationship with God the Father. If He had chosen not to suffer, we would not have this opportunity today.

The same is true in many other situations. If our forefathers had not suffered for freedom, we would not have a nation based on liberty. If the United States had not fought in the Civil War, two World Wars and many other conflicts, we wouldn't enjoy the peace and safety that we know today. There were people who lived for you who never knew you, but they gave to you through their personal suffering. And it could be that your life will demand that you suffer for something that will benefit a whole group of people whom you'll never meet.

Peter said it straight when he wrote in 1 Peter 2:

> But how is it to your credit if you receive a beating for doing wrong and endure it? But if you suffer for doing good and you endure it, this is commendable before God. To this you were called, because Christ suffered for you, leaving you an example, that you should follow in his steps (vv. 20-21).

He repeats the same idea again in chapter 4, when he writes:

If you suffer, it should not be as a murderer or thief or any other kind of criminal, or even as a meddler. However, if you suffer as a Christian, do not be ashamed, but praise God that you bear that name (vv. 15-16).

The book of Revelation puts the icing on the cake regarding this idea. In Revelation 2, the Bible says:

> Do not be afraid of what you are about to suffer. I tell you, the devil will put some of you in prison to test you, and you will suffer persecution for ten days. Be faithful, even to the point of death, and I will give you the crown of life (v. 10).

Christy and Marcus, applying these ideas to your lives will make you people of integrity with incredible character. As you think about them and apply them in daily living, you will find some of the secrets to a great life that many never discover. You'll be able to obey and understand the heart of God. You'll overcome the snares of the world, the deception of the flesh and the schemes of the devil. You will overcome. And when the Bible talks about people like you, here is what it promises:

> To him who *overcomes*, I will give the right to eat from the tree of life, which is in the paradise of God (Rev. 2:7, emphasis added).

> He who *overcomes* will not be hurt at all by the second death (Rev. 2:11, emphasis added).

> To him who *overcomes*, I will give some of the hidden manna. I will also give him a white stone with a new name written on it, known only to him who receives it (Rev. 2:17, emphasis added).

To him who *overcomes* and does my will to the end, I will give authority over the nations—"He will rule them with an iron scepter; he will dash them to pieces like pottery"—just as I have received authority from my Father. I will also give him the morning star (Rev. 2:26-28, emphasis added).

He who *overcomes* will, like them [the people who have not soiled their clothes and walk with God, dressed in white because they are worthy] be dressed in white. I will never blot out his name from the book of life, but will acknowledge his name before my Father and his angels (Rev. 3:5, emphasis added).

He who *overcomes* I will make a pillar in the temple of my God. Never again will he leave it. I will write on him the name of my God and the name of the city of my God, the new Jerusalem, which is coming down out of heaven from my God; and I will also write on him my new name (Rev. 3:12, emphasis added).

To him who *overcomes*, I will give the right to sit with me on my throne, just as I overcame and sat down with my Father on his throne (Rev. 3:21, emphasis added).

He who *overcomes* will inherit all this [the new heaven and the new earth], and I will be his God and he will be my son (Rev. 21:7, emphasis added).

So, Christy and Marcus, it's honorable to acknowledge God before people. It's worth it. I know He's chosen you both to do it.

I love being your dad,

Dad

REFLECTION AND DISCUSSION

1. Does being a Christian have any effect on your relationships?
2. In what ways can you personally acknowledge God in your everyday life?
3. What do you think your actions today communicated about how you feel about God?
4. Are there people in your life who will tell you when your actions are not consistent with your faith?
5. What are the keys to being able to acknowledge God in a pagan culture?

COOPERATE WITH THE HOLY SPIRIT

February 15

Dear Christy and Marcus,

I'll never forget the first time I felt the Holy Spirit touch me. I was a freshman in high school, and a friend of mine had asked me to go with him to a Wednesday night Nazarene church service. I had never been in any type of church other than Presbyterian and assumed that all churches were alike. So when we arrived, I was immediately surprised at the informality of the service—it was more like a prayer meeting and less like the church service I had expected. When prayer began, everyone got onto their knees and prayed out loud, at the same time. What a roar! I never dreamed there could be so much noise in a church. I always knew them to be quiet.

To keep from being conspicuous, I got on my knees and listened to the prayers around me. I heard some people asking for forgiveness, others praying for friends and relatives, and others praying for the people of the city. As I listened, something started to happen to me. For the first time, I thought I felt God. To this day I can't explain exactly what that means, but I just knew that these people were sincere, that they were actually talking to

God and that He was listening. I knew that He was in the room and that He was listening to them and talking to me. Even though the setting was unusual to me, I felt the Spirit touch me.

My friend and I didn't stay long. We left the service and went on our way. I don't remember ever talking about it or even thinking much about it at the time, but to this day when I think of the conviction of the Holy Spirit, my mind goes to Yorktown Nazarene Church in Yorktown, Indiana—the place I first remember being touched by the Holy Spirit

Knowing the Holy Spirit is important. Jesus said in Luke 12:

> Everyone who speaks a word against the Son of Man [Jesus] will be forgiven, but anyone who blasphemes against the Holy Spirit will not be forgiven (v. 10).

In other words, we can be forgiven for everything except blasphemy against the Holy Spirit. If we blaspheme Him, we cannot be forgiven.

But what does that mean? What is "blasphemy"? We don't use that word very often anymore; I usually smile when I hear it because it conjures up images of people of medieval Europe calling one another names—the Catholics were notorious for accusing the Protestants of blasphemy for rejecting the Catholic church's teaching. Blasphemy means to speak negatively about something or someone. It is profane talk, or vilely expressing your rejection of something or someone. To blaspheme is to mock, abuse and malign a person or a teaching. As a purely religious word, it refers to the rejection of God and His teaching. So, to blaspheme the Holy Spirit would be to reject Him, malign Him or mock His work.

Christy and Marcus, movements will come and go within the Church. We can weigh and judge each one carefully, and we may choose to reject some of them. But we must be careful to never reject the Holy Spirit. Jesus is saying that if we speak against the Holy Spirit, we will not be forgiven. So it's important for us to learn how to respect, appreciate and respond rightly to the Holy Spirit. It would be foolish for you to become wealthy or famous or successful in marriage and in other areas of life, but blaspheme the Holy Spirit and end up losing your eternal place with Him. In order to prevent that, you have to become a friend of the Holy Spirit. I want to tell you how to do that by telling you some of my story and showing you some scriptures that relate to the fifth principle for living life successfully:

COOPERATE WITH THE HOLY SPIRIT.

As I mentioned to you in my last letter, after my sophomore year of high school I went to Dallas, Texas, with our youth group and attended a huge Campus Crusade for Christ event, Explo '72, in the big football stadium in Dallas, Texas. On Tuesday night of that week, I sat on the 20-yard line with over 80,000 other high school students and listened to Bill Bright explain the gospel. I understood that I could give my life to Christ and be forgiven of my sins. But I had seen some things in the Church that discouraged me, so I wanted to talk with God a little about this before I prayed to give my life to Christ.

I told God that I didn't want to be like a lot of the Christians I had seen. He said I didn't have to be like any of them. I told God that I wanted a private, personal relationship with Him, a relationship different than the relationship that other people had. He said that was exactly what He wanted. I told Him that if He wanted me to be His, I needed proof that He was going to work with me personally. I said, "If I give my life to You, will You make arrangements so that my roommate doesn't come home early tonight so we can talk as much as we want before I fall asleep?" He said, "Yes."

So I stood up with thousands of other high school students, indicating a commitment to Christ. I could tell that God forgave me of my sins. Rather than feeling relief or elation, I felt sedated. I was contemplative. I rode the bus home and went to my room. All the way home I could hear His voice speaking to me. I could think to Him and He would respond. When I got to my host home, I went to my room and began to pray. I would whisper to God and He would respond with thoughts in my mind. I loved it.

But where was my roommate? I got into bed and whispered to God and He whispered back. This must have gone on for several hours. I'm not sure. All I know is that when my roommate got in, the sun was shining in the window. He had gotten on the wrong bus by mistake and ended up on the wrong side of town and couldn't get back. Another family had taken him in and brought him home to get ready for the day's events.

My prayer was answered. I had tangible proof. I was meeting the Holy Spirit. I didn't know it then, but Jesus said that our relationship with the Holy Spirit would be like this. In John 14, Jesus says:

> And I will ask the Father, and he will give you another Counselor to be with you forever—the Spirit of truth. The world cannot accept him, because it neither sees him nor knows him. But you know him, for he lives with you and will be in you (vv. 16-17).

Well, this happened to me. The Holy Spirit was my Counselor, my Friend, the Spirit of Truth. Once I found this Scripture, I realized that that night the Holy Spirit had become my counselor, my helper, my advisor, my instructor and my teacher. He came near to me. I loved him.

You can imagine how comforted and assured I felt when I first read John 15, where Jesus says:

When the Counselor comes, whom I will send to you from the Father, the Spirit of truth who goes out from the Father, he will testify about me (v. 26).

As I heard Bill Bright speaking that night, I knew that he was telling the truth. As I sat in that Nazarene church listening to those people praying, I knew that they had the truth. And today, as I'm learning to read my Bible and pray, I know I'm still growing in the truth. The Holy Spirit teaches me about Jesus, just as Jesus promised.

Christy and Marcus, I'm sure you have noticed the futility of trying to find truth without the guidance of the Holy Spirit. People look to mystics, seances, the stars, palm readers and false religion, and they make all sorts of other awkward attempts to figure out the meaning of life. But it can't be done. It's impossible. God must reveal Himself to people by His Spirit according to the Scriptures. It is a mystery—one that we must embrace as we trust the Holy Spirit.

Many who call themselves Christians do not have a revelation of Christ from the Scriptures. Many who call themselves Christian scholars don't have the Holy Spirit teaching them. God has to show you His truth as you pray and study the Bible. In order to know Christ truly, deeply and clearly, you need a friendship with the Holy Spirit and a love for the Scriptures. Somehow this balance opens the gates of heaven for you, so you can know Him and His power, which will make you great spouses, workers, parents, citizens and thinkers. God will show the way.

When I went to college, I heard about the baptism in the Holy Spirit and the gifts of the Spirit still at work in the lives of believers today. I appreciated those ideas, but didn't like the fact that people had taken it past what I believed were biblical parameters. There were constant, heated disagreements about this sort of thing, so I spent a good deal of time studying the Scriptures in order to help people learn strong, sound doctrine, so they could have a healthy and balanced biblical perspective.

The position I took was that the gifts had ceased in the Church, either when the last apostle died or when the canon of the Scriptures was complete. I believed this, knew the arguments and taught them strongly. The best place from which to argue this was 1 Corinthians 13, where Paul writes:

> But where there are prophecies, they will cease; where there are tongues, they will be stilled; where there is knowledge, it will pass away (v. 8).

To me, this demonstrated clearly that the gifts are temporary.

After a while, though, I realized that in order to teach this position I had to randomly separate Scripture. From 1 Corinthians 13:8, for example, I taught that prophecy and tongues had passed away, but knowledge hadn't. In Ephesians 4:11, the Bible says: "It was he who gave some to be apostles, some to be prophets, some to be evangelists, and some to be pastors and teachers." I taught that we didn't need apostles and prophets any longer, but we did have evangelists, pastors and teachers.

This random and illogical separation of the Scriptures went on and on. In Romans 12, Paul writes:

> We have different gifts, according to the grace given us. If a man's gift is prophesying, let him use it in proportion to his faith. If it is serving, let him serve; if it is teaching, let him teach; if it is encouraging, let him encourage; if it is contributing to the needs of others, let him give gener-

ously; if it is leadership, let him govern diligently; if it is showing mercy, let him do it cheerfully (vv. 6-8).

I taught that all of these gifts of the Holy Spirit were available except the gift of prophesy. Why? I began to question my own interpretation, but it still seemed fairly reasonable and very few people tested me on it.

I didn't just separate verses—I separated entire chapters. When I taught 1 Corinthians, I would teach up through chapter 11 and then tell people that chapters 12 and 14 didn't apply any longer, so we didn't need to study them. I would emphasize the theme of love in chapter 13 and continue the study with chapter 15. I did not believe that the Holy Spirit had any other gifts for believers except the gift of eternal life.

It seemed clear to me that the gifts of the Holy Spirit were given to validate who Christ was. Hebrews 2 says:

God also testified to it [salvation through Christ alone] by signs, wonders and various miracles, and gifts of the Holy Spirit distributed according to his will (v. 4).

Since we have the Bible, it never dawned on me that there were people all over the world who still need the testimony of the gospel validated through the power of the Holy Spirit.

I regret it now, but I believed then that those who practiced the gifts of the Spirit were weak-minded, poorly trained, or influenced by demonic doctrine or demons themselves. I knew that if people would simply study the Word, they would understand what Christ had to offer them. They didn't need all these experiences they were claiming to have. In my view, charismatic teaching was a distraction.

But then, slowly, my perspective began to change. I studied John 20:22 and learned how that verse tells about the disciples first receiving the Holy Spirit. The setting is after the resurrection and just prior to Jesus' ascension into heaven. The disciples already had their names written in heaven (Luke 10:20) and they knew the Lord personally (obviously; they had been living with Him for three years). Then, John 20:22 says: "And with that [the Lord Jesus sending them as He was sent] he breathed on them and said, 'Receive the Holy Spirit.'"

When Jesus did this, it happened in that moment. This was not a prophecy looking forward to a future time when they would receive the Spirit. This verse is very clear: He breathed on them, and they received the Holy Spirit. As I read this verse and studied it in its original language, it became evident that the disciples received the Holy Spirit at this point.

Then, in Acts 1 Jesus told these same people:

> Do not leave Jerusalem, but wait for the gift my Father promised, which you have heard me speak about. For John baptized with water, but in a few days you will be baptized with the Holy Spirit (vv. 4-5).

What gift could Jesus have been talking about? The gift of eternal life? They already had it. The gift of knowing Christ personally? They already knew Him. The gift of the indwelling Holy Spirit? No, that was recorded already in John 20:22.

He's talking about a baptism in the Holy Spirit. The word "baptism" is simple. It means to dip or immerse. Jesus is saying that just as we can be immersed in water to indicate our repentance, we can be immersed in the Holy Spirit.

Clearly, the Bible was speaking about two experiences involving the Holy Spirit, not one. First, the Holy Spirit comes into us when we turn away from our old lives and ask Christ to build His life in us. That's when we become a Christian. We are new creations and are born again, and we have the Holy Spirit.

He lives in us and, if we welcome Him, He will dominate our lives.

The second is a total immersion in the Holy Spirit through a supernatural baptism. This baptism occurred for the first time in Acts 2. Because it happened on the Jewish holiday of Pentecost, people who highlight this event in their doctrine are sometimes called Pentecostals. The Bible records the experience as follows:

> When the Day of Pentecost came, they were all together in one place. Suddenly a sound like the blowing of a violent wind came from heaven and filled the whole house where they were sitting. They saw what seemed to be tongues of fire that separated and came to rest on each of them. All of them were filled with the Holy Spirit and began to speak in other tongues as the Spirit enabled them (vv. 1-4).

There are several strong ideas here for you to catch:

1. *The blowing of a violent wind.*
In the Bible, the image of wind is often used in reference to God's Spirit. The wind here is associated with the way the Holy Spirit leads us where God wants us to go. In John 3, when Jesus describes the work of the Spirit in our lives, He says:

> You should not be surprised at my saying, "You must be born again." The wind blows wherever it pleases. You hear its sound, but you cannot tell where it comes from or where it is going. So it is with everyone born of the Spirit (vv. 7-8).

2. *Tongues of fire.*
The fire is a picture of the way the Holy Spirit purifies our lives. When John the Baptist was prophesying about this event, he said:

I baptize you with water for repentance. But after me will come one who is more powerful than I, whose sandals I am not fit to carry. He will baptize you with the Holy Spirit and with fire (Matt. 3:11).

3.   *Filled with the Holy Spirit.*

Even though these disciples had already received the Holy Spirit, now they were being filled with the Holy Spirit so their witness could be strengthened. We see this direct correlation again in Acts 4, where the Bible says:

After they prayed, the place where they were meeting was shaken. And they were all filled with the Holy Spirit and spoke the word of God boldly (v. 31).

4.   *Speaking in other tongues.*

The term tongues is used here and other places in the New Testament in reference to other languages. In 1 Corinthians 13:1, the apostle Paul says that when people speak in other languages through the power of the Holy Spirit, they may be speaking in the language of another group of people here on the earth or an angelic language. He writes: "If I speak in the tongues *of men and of angels,* but have not love, I am only a resounding gong or clanging cymbal" (emphasis added).

Why is this useful for us? Well, we don't always know how to pray for the perfect will of God, so speaking in tongues is allowing the Holy Spirit to pray through us. Paul explained it this way:

We do not know what we ought to pray for, but the Spirit himself intercedes for us with groans that words cannot express. And he who searches our hearts knows the mind of the Spirit, because the Spirit intercedes for the saints in accordance with God's will (Rom. 8:26-27).

When I studied all of this closely, I began to wonder seriously about the ideas I had been teaching. I sincerely believed that
when we were born again we received everything we would ever
need to receive. But now I saw two vivid experiences in the Early
Church. I set it aside for a few months to think about it.

As I continued to read the Bible, I came across Acts 19, where
Paul meets some people who have believed in Christ and have
been water baptized. He asks them if they have also received the
Holy Spirit, and they say no. So, Paul prays for them to receive.
Acts 19:6 tells us: "When Paul placed his hands on them, the
Holy Spirit came on them, and they spoke in tongues and
prophesied."

Even though I didn't believe in the modern need for tongues
or prophecy, I clearly saw two experiences. But I didn't tell anyone, and I continued to teach that when you give your life to
Christ, you have received all that you will ever receive.

Then one night a friend of mine who had a strong background in Bible memory through the Navigator ministry and
had served as a Christian leader for years asked me to go with
him while he prayed to be baptized in the Holy Spirit. I still
didn't believe in that, but I did know that the general ministry of
the Holy Spirit was important for all Christians. So, while he
prayed to be baptized in the Holy Spirit, I prayed that God
would touch him and would protect him from deception. In the
process of that prayer, he didn't receive anything unusual—but
I did! The Holy Spirit came upon me in a special way, and
I received a prayer language that I hadn't learned. It edified me.
It built me up spiritually. It made me rejoice in God, it made me
want to be obedient to everything God wanted me to do and
caused me to feel strong in my relationship with Christ. That
night, I was dipped in the Holy Spirit. I was immersed in God.

Because of what happened to me, I began to understand that
all of the ministries of the Holy Spirit operate today. We still

have apostolic ministry: powerful missionary outreaches that effectively penetrate the darkest areas of the world. We still have prophetic ministry: ministries that clearly articulate the Word of God for us. We still experience signs and wonders: The resurrection of Jesus is validated through miracles to those who have no context for a risen Lord. As I travel all over the world, I see virtually everything the New Testament talks about continuing today, and that is how the gospel is spreading as rapidly as it is. The Holy Spirit works today just as He did 2,000 years ago.

I no longer divide verses randomly. First Corinthians 13 clearly says that tongues, prophecy and knowledge will cease "when perfection comes" and when we see Him "face to face" (vv. 10,12). These gifts are certainly all imperfect right now, but Jesus, who is perfection, will render them useless when He returns. So now, the Scriptures that I used to ignore have come alive. Now 1 Corinthians 12 and 14 mean something powerful for all of us. The New Testament Church is *now*. Jesus is resurrected from the dead, and we can all be filled with His power.

So what does the Bible say about the Holy Spirit?

> He conceived God's plan in Mary and Elizabeth, and wants to plant God's plan in us (see Matt. 1:18,20; Luke 1:35,41).
>
> Jesus baptizes us in Him (see Matt. 3:11; Mark 1:8; Luke 3:16; John 1:33; Acts 1:5; 2:33).
>
> Because He is God's Spirit, if you reject His work, you cannot find forgiveness from God (see Matt. 12:32; Mark 3:29; Luke 12:10).
>
> New believers are to be baptized in water in His name (see Matt. 28:19).
>
> He speaks (see Mark 12:36; 13:11; Luke 1:67; Acts 1:16; 4:8, 25; 13:2; 21:11; 28:25; Heb. 3:7; 10:15; 1 Pet. 1:12; 2 Pet. 1:21).

He filled John the Baptist, Jesus, Simeon and others. And
He wants to fill us (see Luke 1:15; 2:25; Acts 4:31; 6:5;
7:55; 9:17; 13:52).

He teaches (see Luke 2:26; 12:12; John 14:26; Acts 1:2;
Heb. 9:8).

He leads (see Luke 4:1; Acts 13:4; 16:6; 20:23).

He gives joy (see John 17:13; Rom. 14:17; 1 Thess. 1:6).

He's given by the Father to those who ask (see Luke 11:13).

He must be received so we can be born again (see John
20:22; Titus 3:5-6).

He must be received so believers can be empowered
(see Luke 3:22; Acts 1:8; 8:14-17; 13:9-11; 19:2-7;
Rom. 15:13).

He gives believers the ability to pray and declare God's
wonders (see Acts 2:4; Rom. 8:26-27; Jude 20).

He gives gifts to believers (see Acts 2:38; Rom. 12:6-8;
1 Cor. 12:4-11; Heb. 2:4).

God indwells, adopts and takes ownership of people
through the Holy Spirit (see John 14:17; Rom. 8:15;
2 Cor. 1:22; Eph. 1:13-14).

He can be resisted (see Acts 7:51).

He cannot be purchased (see Acts 8:18-23).

He gives strength and encouragement (see Acts 9:31).

He anoints for ministry (see Acts 10:38; 11:24).

He comes upon people in response to the gospel (see
Acts 10:44-47; Acts 11:15-21).

He is a deposit and the seal of God in our hearts that
guarantees our eternal inheritance (see Acts 15:8;
Eph. 1:13).

He has opinions (see Acts 15:28).

He gives spiritual authority (see Acts 20:28).

He delivers God's love into our hearts (see Rom. 5:5).

He confirms God's will (see Rom. 9:1).

He works God's kingdom into our hearts (see Rom. 14:17).

He sets us apart to God (see Rom. 15:16).

He dwells in us, making us the temple and property of
   God (see 1 Cor. 6:19).

He proclaims the Lordship of Jesus (see 1 Cor. 12:3).

All believers must be in Him (see 2 Cor. 6:6).

All believers can fellowship with Him (see 2 Cor. 13:14).

He can be grieved (see Eph. 4:30).

He confirms the gospel (see 1 Thess. 1:5).

God gives Him to us (see 1 Thess. 4:8).

He helps us (see 2 Tim. 1:14).

He renews us (see Titus 3:5).

These are a few of the things the Holy Spirit does. There are many more. Study this list, look up the verses and ask God to cause His Spirit to edify and teach you.

As you study, you'll see that if we learn to cooperate with the Holy Spirit, our lives will be incredible. If, on the other hand, we choose to blatantly disregard and rebel against the ministry of a kind of the Holy Spirit rejecting His testimony and maligning His work, we're guilty of a kind blasphemy which can never be forgiven.

But why would anyone want to reject the ministry of the Holy Spirit? He is so good! He is so wonderful! That's why the Bible says that we are to earnestly desire spiritual gifts (see 1 Cor. 14:1). I think it's good to earnestly desire everything that God has to offer—absolutely everything.

Am I saying that you've got to speak in tongues or operate in the gifts to know Christ, be saved or even be spiritfilled? No. But I am saying that the Holy Spirit is the One who leads us into everything that is eternally good, so we should never reject His voice, shun His leading or resist His call. To do so would lead us where we don't want to go.

Why is rejecting the ministry of the Holy Spirit the "unpardonable sin" (see Matt. 12:31-32)? Because it's the Holy Spirit who convicts us of our sins and draws us to Christ (see John 16:7-11). Jesus is God's only provision for eternal life. So if a person rejects the ministry of the Holy Spirit, they will ultimately deny Christ and shut the door on salvation. On the other hand, when we cooperate with the Holy Spirit we are drawn toward Christ and can receive His gift of eternal life.

So I encourage you: Study the Scriptures about the Holy Spirit, and learn His voice, be filled and empowered and live by His strength. As you do these things, you'll be strong, victorious and enriched—for all eternity. You can't beat that!

I love being your dad,

REFLECTION AND DISCUSSION

1. What does it mean to become a friend of the Holy Spirit?
2. How does cooperating with the Holy Spirit relate to the earlier principles of success discussed in these letters?
3. How does separating the Scriptures lead you into error? Can you think of a time when you realized that the Scriptures were connected in a meaningful, powerful way?
4. How would you describe the phrase "filled with the Holy Spirit" to another believer? To a nonbeliever?
5. Read through two or three of the verses about the Holy Spirit that are listed in this letter. What do those Scriptures teach you about the Spirit's work?

MAINTAIN POWER UNDER PRESSURE

February 19

Dear Christy and Marcus,

Last night your mom and I stayed up late watching a special on CNN about former president Ronald Reagan. What an incredible life he has lived! When Reagan was elected, the United States was struggling with low morale because of high interest rates, unemployment and taxes. But after his election, he stood strong, working hard to persuade people that he could help relieve the pressure. Then he ended the cold war, slashed taxes to strengthen the economy and got unemployment under control. Americans were again pleased to be citizens.

How did this happen? Because Ronald Reagan was willing to stand outside of the pack in order to make a difference. He didn't just go along with the crowd; he stood apart and worked for the good.

Of course, people who stand apart from the crowd aren't always the best people. Everyone who makes a difference, whether for good or evil, is someone who stands outside the crowd. Those who simply go along with the crowd never impact others significantly. But if people can find the strength to break out of the group, they are positioned to make a difference—whether good or bad.

Some say that you can learn the history of the entire twentieth century by reading the biographies of seven men. Think of that. *Seven* people were the key influencers in the twentieth century: Vladimir Lenin, Joseph Stalin, Adolf Hitler, Mao Tse-tung, Theodore Roosevelt, Winston Churchill and Ronald Reagan. Four of these men were tyrants, three of them heroes. But each of them stood strong under pressure and changed the way millions of people lived their lives. Other twentieth century heroes such as Martin Luther King, Jr., Mother Teresa and Mahatma Gandhi are also notable because they developed a set of core beliefs, communicated them well and thus changed our world.

Jesus emphasized the necessity of being willing to stand out from the crowd and depend on the Holy Spirit to help in time of need. He said, in Luke 12,

> When you are brought before synagogues, rulers and authorities, do not worry about how you will defend yourselves or what you will say, for the Holy Spirit will teach you at that time what you should say (vv. 11-12).

Jesus is making several points. First, He assumes that His followers will be in situations where they will be in potential trouble and will have to answer for themselves. Second, He also assumes that His followers will be strong and walk through the process. And third, He says that the Holy Spirit will assist them and give them the words to speak. This highlights the sixth principle for successful living that I want to explain to you:

MAINTAIN POWER UNDER PRESSURE.

As I mentioned in my earlier letters, I became a Christian at a time when a large number of Christians were suffering because of communism. In my early years as a Christian, I was saturated with stories of pastors being killed or imprisoned, parents being jailed for teaching their children that there was a God and churches being bulldozed down—often with worshippers inside. Frequently these stories of martyrdom would include accounts of heroes standing for their faith in the midst of terror. These accounts always gave us faith and confidence in the Lord and spurred us on to greater service.

Now that you are growing and becoming mature, it's time for you to make some decisions about the type of person you are going to be. Will you stand alone if necessary? Will you stick up for principles and ideals, even if it may cost you imprisonment or potentially your life? Do you stand for anything? Are you doing the things you need to do to grow in strength, or are you doing things that will ultimately make you weaker?

In Luke 12, Jesus is saying that if you ever have to face a time of great pressure or stand alone for your beliefs and convictions, He will be with you by His Spirit and give you the strength and the words you need. Certainly I hope you never have to face danger, but it is very important that you make the decision in advance about what your response will be, so that if a difficult circumstance develops, you've already chosen to have character and inner strength.

Two significant Old Testament characters are remembered for their decisions to stand alone: Abraham and Moses. Abraham had to leave everything to pursue his walk of obedience. Moses had to maintain a strong perspective in the midst of pressure from every side to become the great deliverer that we still appreciate so much today. In the New Testament, if Jesus hadn't been willing to be ostracized (even from God!), we wouldn't know God in a personal, intimate way today. And if the apostle Paul had refused to take blows for the gospel, we Gentiles wouldn't know the gospel today. The world is formed by those who know how to stand strong, even when standing alone.

This past January the El Paso County Ministerial Union invited me to be the speaker for the Martin Luther King, Jr. celebration at New Jerusalem Baptist Church. In that talk, I told the crowd that there were two African-American men who stood out to me for their courage and strength. One was George Washington Carver; the other was Martin Luther King, Jr. Both were self-made men who pursued big ideas that changed our history and made them great. Because of these men and their ability to face adversity, our nation enjoys more freedom today than we had a generation ago.

I first became aware of George Washington Carver when I was in the fourth grade. My teacher gave me a book about him that I read over and over again. I vividly remember a picture in the book of him kneeling in the woods, praying. That image was planted so deeply in me that I believed that no matter what the circumstances were, if a person would seek God and learn from Him, God could do miracles through them. And God did do miracles through George Washington Carver.

Carver was born to a slave girl near Diamond Grove, Missouri, during some of the worst years of slavery in the United States. Bigotry, hatred and racial discrimination were actually encouraged during his lifetime. But this man was able to maintain a godly innocence that propelled him toward great success.

As a child, Carver was a sponge for learning. He had exceptional observational skills and a keen curiosity about nature and animals. Because he was black, he wasn't allowed to attend school with white children, so he had to attend a separate school with other African-American kids in another city away from his family. Think of the rejection and ridicule he must have endured. He could have easily given up or claimed that he was a victim of social inequality, which he was. But he had something inside him that made him great in the midst of struggle.

As a result of his godly response and determination to learn, he was admitted to Iowa State University in 1891 and received his bachelor's degree in 1894. In 1897, he received a master's degree in bacterial botany and agriculture. But for Carver, it wasn't as simple as enrolling in school, taking the classes and getting the degrees. Since he never had enough money to pay his fees, Carver would often have to drop out of school temporarily to earn the money to reenroll. He worked as a housekeeper, cook, gardener and laundryman, and they say he did every job with devotion and tried to achieve perfection. In the midst of his work, studies and severe discrimination, he took art and piano lessons. Because he could maintain his composure and direction while under pressure, he gained recognition everywhere he went. How? Because others were normal, average and submissive to their environment, while he remained strong.

I know some of these details might not interest you, but think of this man's great accomplishments: Before affirmative action, school loans and government programs for the underprivileged, Carver was able to sustain strength, dignity and innocence. He maintained power and confidence under extreme pressure.

Carver was the first African-American teacher at Iowa State University. In 1897, Booker T. Washington, founder of the Tuskegee Institute, convinced him to serve there. Carver agreed and was there until his death in 1943. He died an incredible man who was never stained by the negative atmosphere of his culture. He stood tall. He said, "I will never let another man ruin my life by making me hate him." He was a committed Christian with a deep understanding of the importance of a clean heart. Even though many in his generation said a black man would not be allowed to achieve, he did. How? Because he knew something most others don't. He understood true success. He trusted the Holy Spirit to see him through and help him think and speak clearly.

Even back then, he was helping people live a better life. He encouraged people to recycle things like bottles, pots, wires and tubes from the trash and converted them to lab equipment. He would not allow people to whine or bemoan their conditions and never tolerated blaming others for negative conditions. As a Christian, he felt that every day offered a new opportunity to make life better. When farmers were harvesting cotton and tobacco crops year after year and depleting the soil, he taught them about plant rotation with peanuts and sweet potatoes. As a result, crops improved. At the time, there wasn't a strong market for peanuts and sweet potatoes, but Carver changed that too by developing products from peanuts and sweet potatoes—some of which you use today. He made peanut butter, shampoo, milk, cheese, mayonnaise, instant coffee, flour, soap, dyes, face powder, oil, adhesives, plastics and pickles out of peanuts. From sweet potatoes he made vinegar, flour, starch, ink and molasses. In all, he developed 325 products from peanuts, 108 products from sweet potatoes, 75 products from pecan, 118 industrial products from agricultural products and over 500 dyes from plants. He changed the entire agricultural base of the South. Because of Carver, poor farmers became prosperous.

As a result of his achievements, he received an honorary doctorate from Simpson College in 1928, was made an honorary member of the Royal Society of Arts in London, England, and was awarded the Roosevelt Medal for restoring southern agriculture. When he died, Franklin Roosevelt honored him with a national monument dedicated to his accomplishments.

Now you see why I love this man. He said, "It is not the style of clothes one wears, neither the kind of automobile one drives, nor the amount of money one has in the bank that counts.

These mean nothing. It is simply service that measures success."

If George Washington Carver hadn't had the internal convictions and strength to stand alone, America could have taken a different track. We can only imagine how often George Washington Carver must have prayed for God to give him the right words and ideas to improve the plight of people in trouble.

Another man who had this same strength is Martin Luther King, Jr. I think he, more than any other African-American man in history, pushed our nation forward in the direction of racial justice.

He was born in the home of Pastor and Mrs. Martin Luther King in Atlanta, Georgia. In 1944 he graduated from Booker T. Washington High School, but he didn't stop there. (Christy and Marcus, I want you to see that both George Washington Carver and Martin Luther King, Jr., had something burning inside of them. Somehow they knew that education and spirituality were important. Somehow they knew that life could be improved, but not without taking the risk to believe something and be willing to stand strong for it.) Born to a poor African-American pastor and his wife, before affirmative action programs, in the midst of harsh Jim Crow laws that provided government endorsement to racism, Martin Luther King, Jr., found a way to get a strong education. He graduated from Morehouse College in 1948 and went straight to seminary to complete a Ph.D. in systematic theology from Boston University.

No one *gave* him his degree. No one coddled him. He had something inside of him that reminded him of God's view of mankind and the need to confront injustice. He was no slacker, whiner or wimp. And even though he had horrible obstacles to overcome, he did it without the assistance of others. He stood tall in his own shoes. He worked hard. In 1957, he traveled 780,000 miles and made 208 speeches, many of them to small crowds. And the work paid off. God gave him a dream.

When he said that he'd been to the mountaintop, he meant it. He studied and loved theology and his speeches were saturated with insight into the way God's principles can improve the human condition. He confronted evil with an innocent determination that couldn't be stopped. The understanding he gained from growing up in a pastor's home, prayer, the Bible and seminary kept his enemies from finding a handle from which they could pull him down. He was never defeated. He won. His ideas prevailed.

Martin Luther King, Jr., provided much of the leadership that led to the Civil Rights Act of 1958 and 1964 and the Voting Rights Act of 1965. He was the youngest person ever to win the Nobel Peace Prize (he was 35) and was *Time Magazine*'s "Man of the Year" in 1964. This guy was incredible! He was ordained as a Baptist pastor at 19. He pastored Dexter Avenue Baptist Church in Montgomery before pastoring with his dad at Ebenezer Baptist Church in Atlanta. At his freedom walk in 1963, 125,000 people joined him; 250,000 people were in Washington, D.C., for his "I Have A Dream" speech. It's no wonder that America celebrates his birth on January 20th.

Martin Luther King, Jr., was not without fault, but God used his willingness to stand apart from the crowd to radically change our country. He was a person just like you are. He wasn't perfect, but he did achieve his goal. This is why he is one of my heroes.

One of my favorite quotes from Dr. King is "Darkness cannot drive out darkness; only light can do that. Hate cannot drive out hate; only love can do that."[1]

Here are a few other great quotes from Martin Luther King, Jr. Read them closely, and try to see the spirit in him that caused him to stand out from the crowd and stand firm in his convictions, even in the midst of rejection, hatred and imprisonment:

It is quite easy for me to think of a God of love mainly because I grew up in a family where love was central and where lovely relationships were ever present . . . religion has been real to me and closely knitted to life. In fact, the two cannot be separated; religion for me is life.[2]

A just law is a man-made code that squares with the moral law or the law of God. An unjust law is a code that is out of harmony with the moral law. To put it in the terms of Saint Thomas Aquinas, an unjust law is a human law that is not rooted in eternal and natural law.[3]

We cannot be truly Christian people so long as we flaunt the central teachings of Jesus: brotherly love and the Golden Rule.[4]

In his determination to defend his extreme position on the cause of justice, he wrote while jailed in Birmingham:

Was not Jesus an extremist for love? "Love your enemies, bless them that curse you, pray for them that despitefully use you."

Was not Amos an extremist for justice? "Let justice roll down like waters and righteousness like a mighty stream."

Was not Paul an extremist for the gospel of Jesus Christ? "I bear in my body the marks of the Lord Jesus."

Was not John Bunyan an extremist? "I will stay in jail to the end of my days before I make a butchery of my conscience."

Was not Abraham Lincoln an extremist? "This nation cannot survive half slave and half free."

Was not Thomas Jefferson an extremist? "We hold these truths to be self-evident, that all men are created equal."

So the question is not whether we will be extremist, but what kind of extremist will we be? Will we be extremists for hate, or will we be extremists for love? Will we be extremists for the preservation of injustice—or will we be extremists for the cause of justice? In that dramatic scene on Calvary's hill, three men were crucified. We must not forget that all three were crucified for the same crime—the crime of extremism. Two were extremists for immorality, and thusly fell below their environment. The other, Jesus Christ, was an extremist for love, truth and goodness, and thereby rose above his environment.[5]

Christy and Marcus, something great happens in people when they discover their resolve. I know you have memorized many Martin Luther King quotes that are more famous than the ones I've listed here for you, but I wanted you to have the ones that communicated not just his ideals, but reveal his core resolve. From the Birmingham jail he also wrote this paragraph that challenges all of us to be salt and light, to break out of the crowd and help humanity think and live well.

There was a time when the Church was very powerful. It was during that period when the early Christians rejoiced when they were deemed worthy to suffer for what they believed. In those days the Church was not merely a thermometer that recorded the ideas and principles of popular opinion; it was a thermostat that transformed the mores of society. Whenever the early Christians entered a town the power structure got disturbed and immediately sought to convict them for being "disturbers of the peace" and "outside agitators." But they went on with the conviction that they were "a colony of heaven," and had to obey God rather than man. They were small in number but big in commitment. They were too God-intoxicated to be "astronomically intimidated." They brought an end to such ancient evils as infanticide and gladiatorial contest.[6]

They changed the world, and you can too.

I just read a book by David Gergen entitled *Eyewitness to Power*. David Gergen has been closely involved with presidential leadership here in the United States for most of his adult life. He was close to the White House under Richard Nixon, Gerald Ford, Jimmy Carter, Ronald Reagan, George Bush and Bill Clinton, and so has gained a bright grasp of leadership. After serving with most of these men and observing them all, he found six lessons of leadership that I think apply to successful leaders, both of nations as well as of families. I want to share the lessons of leadership with you, some directly from Gergen's book and others modified slightly so they apply to you:

1. *Leadership starts from within.*

At the core of every significant leader is a belief or philosophy that causes them to burn for a cause. Abraham believed God and it changed the world. Moses saw a burning bush and moral law was the result. Paul was transformed on the way to Damascus and made faith available to all Gentiles. Each of these men, and every other leader of quality, had something inside them that made them worth listening to.

Interestingly, when we think of the seven most influential personalities of the twentieth century (again: Lenin, Stalin, Hitler, Mao Tse-tung, Roosevelt, Churchill and Reagan), all of them probably thought they were doing a good thing for their followers and for the world. But now we know that four of them were such harsh tyrants that if Roosevelt and Churchill hadn't rallied the West, and Reagan hadn't finished the task by winning the Cold War, we might not have civilization today. Each of them believed something in the core of their being and communicated it to the best of their ability. They formed the world that we live in today.

So what about you and me? Well, we need to come to a place of resolve where we are informed, good and influential. We need to help our generation move forward instead of backward. We need to have integrity so our actions validate our beliefs. We need to lead from the core of our lives.

2. *Leaders must have a central, compelling purpose.*
In order for our lives to make a difference, we have to know where we are in time, what God's plan is for our generation and what our role might be in that plan. Previous generations have had to topple tyrants, establish justice for all and create equal opportunity for education. What a tragedy it would have been if Lincoln hadn't realized his role in our nation or if Rembrandt had been a carpenter instead of an artist. What if Michelangelo had become a rancher or if George Washington had become a boat captain? Roles are important, and we have to know what we are created to do.

There is nothing so horrible as a wasted life. And since the Bible tells us that every human being is made in the image and likeness of God, then you are created by God to make the world a better place for at least one person, and hopefully for many. But you've got to know His will, His plan and His desire, and you can only find that by seeking Him.

Four years ago I wrote a book entitled *Primary Purpose*. That book was designed to assist people in finding their purpose and direction in life. God doesn't want anyone to waste their lives and find themselves at the end of their days bemoaning the fact that they didn't improve humanity. As I write, Ronald Reagan is 90 years old. Because he has Alzheimer's disease he isn't aware of his impact, but I am sitting in my easy chair in a safe country under a freely elected government working in a free-market economy because of Ronald Reagan. He insured that we wouldn't have to lose in a nuclear holocaust all that had been earned. It cost us more money than we had to spend, but it might have saved our lives.

This was his role. This was his purpose. Just as Mother Teresa's purpose was to help the poor in the streets of Calcutta, and my purpose is to pastor the people who attend our church, and your mother's purpose is to train women and colabor with me in parenting you. Discovering purpose is discovering happiness.

3. *Leaders must have a capacity to persuade.*

Every person I've referred to in this chapter and every person who has captured your attention in a significant way has done so because he or she learned to persuade others. So often we hear people talk about the value of independence and freedom from others. But we all impact others whether we know it or not, so it's a skill to learn to persuade others to do the right thing, to reach higher and to run further. To assist another in thinking well is a gift too. I think the two of you have it.

4. *Leaders must have the ability to work within a system— or build a better one.*

The best leaders must first learn to be good followers. Many good people have never been able to have much influence because they never developed the ability to work within a system. Far too often, people become overly critical of systems and institutions, and they spend so much time complaining that they never get any work done. But not one of the presidents of the United States, senators, congressmen or even city council members could serve publicly if they couldn't work within systems. You can't even be a church member if you can't work within systems. Really, you can't do anything unless you can work within a system.

Christy and Marcus, study systems, learn them well, and use them to benefit others.

5. *Leaders must find and keep strong, prudent friends and advisors.*
I believe that one of the greatest gifts that we have been given as a family are the friends and advisors who give us strength and help us think. All of us should intentionally identify people we admire and do everything within our power to learn from them. Right now, you are reading this in order to gain some insight that will make you more successful in life. When I finish writing this letter, I'll either pick up a magazine or a book and read for a while before going to bed. Why? Because I want to know what others are saying and thinking. Tomorrow I'll go to the office and at some point in the course of the day I'll meet with some of the members of our executive leadership team. Why? Because they will provide advice about the decisions that have to be made, and if they are strong and prudent and I heed their counsel, then my life will produce more tomorrow than it would have otherwise.

The book of Proverbs says there are two women crying in the streets for our attention. One is folly and the other is wisdom (compare chapters 7 and 8). Our goal is to find wisdom through prayer, the Scriptures, trusted friends and advisors. We must avoid the worldview of a fool, through which we would waste the life God has given us and find ourselves in despair as the years pass.

6. *Leaders must be able to inspire others to carry on the mission.*
George Washington Carver and Dr. Martin Luther King, Jr., are both dead, but we value their lives, we believe their words, and we want to follow their mission to insure it's not lost in our generation. Abraham, Moses, Jesus and Paul gave their lives centuries

ago and we're still moved by their legacies. So the question is—what about us? What are we doing? What are we saying? Will people remember our mission?

Christy and Marcus, in order to lead you have to live lives that stand out. Don't be normal. Use your places of leadership to serve others. God might use you to reach millions, like the people I've referenced in this letter, or He might use you to help just one. Either of these callings is equally worthy if you do it well. Break out of the pack and depend upon Him to give you the ideas and words, and you'll do very well in life.

I love being your dad,

REFLECTION AND DISCUSSION

1. Can you think of a time when you had to stand apart from the crowd? How did it make you feel, and how did things turn out?
2. Think of a hard decision you've made that helped you be a stronger person.
3. If someone asked you today what your purpose in life was, what would you say?
4. What person do you admire the most and why? What can you learn from them?
5. List all of the books you have read in the last year—required reading doesn't count! Are they good books? Do you need to enlarge your scope of interest?
6. Why are systems important to lasting influence?

Notes

1. Martin Luther King, Jr., "The Strength to Love," in *A Testament of Hope: The Essential Speeches and Writings of Martin Luther King, Jr.*, ed. James M. Washington (San Francisco: Harper San Francisco, 1994), n.p.

2. Martin Luther King, Jr., "An Autobiography of Religious Development," November 1950 essay.

3. Martin Luther King, Jr., "Letter from the Birmingham City Jail," in *A Testament of Hope*, n.p.

4. Martin Luther King, Jr., "The Negro and the Constitution," *The Cornellian* (May 1944), n.p.

5. Martin Luther King, Jr., "Letter from the Birmingham City Jail," in *A Testament of Hope*, n.p.

6. Ibid., n.p.

BECOME RICH
TOWARD GOD

February 22

Dear Christy and Marcus,

You're old enough now to have learned a thing or two about money. You know that it can feel like there's never enough of it, that it runs out before you think it will and that it can bring you and others a certain amount of pleasure and safety if it's handled well. Marcus, you've learned that it takes money to support your love of music and 4x4s. Christy, you've learned that money comes in handy when you want a horse or a beautiful dog to show. Money matters.

Money can be a wonderful blessing or a terrible curse, depending on the choices that you make. Right now, there is more money in the world than ever before. People in America are producing things more efficiently and earning more income than at any point in human history. Overall, there is an unprecedented abundance. But at the same time, people are still starving; some folks, including those in retirement, don't have any savings and many families all over the country are living from hand to mouth, hoping to make ends meet. What separates the haves from the have-nots? How do some people figure out how to make money work for them, while others spend their entire lives working for money?

As your father, it's so important for me to help you understand how to make money a blessing for you and those around you. Far too many people ruin their lives because of money, and it doesn't have to be that way. There is a lot of good, practical advice available on how to use money wisely, and I want you to be familiar with that material. More importantly though, I want you to follow a piece of biblical advice that will protect you from ever getting trapped in a financial tragedy:

BECOME RICH TOWARD GOD.

Jesus addressed this issue in (you guessed it!) Luke 12. Luke writes:

> Someone in the crowd said to him, "Teacher, tell my brother to divide the inheritance with me." Jesus replied, "Man, who appointed me a judge or an arbiter between you?" Then he said to them, "Watch out! Be on your guard against all kinds of greed; a man's life does not consist in the abundance of his possessions." And he told them this parable: "The ground of a certain rich man produced a good crop. He thought to himself, 'What shall I do? I have no place to store my crops.' Then he said, 'This is what I'll do. I will tear down my barns and build bigger ones, and there I will store all my grain and my goods. And I'll say to myself, "You have plenty of good things laid up for many years. Take life easy; eat, drink and be merry."'
>
> "But God said to him, 'You fool! This very night your life will be demanded from you. Then who will get what

you have prepared for yourself?' This is how it will be with anyone who stores up things for himself *but is not rich toward God*" (vv. 13-21, emphasis added).

Every time I talk about this subject, there are a few people who think this illustration shows that God is against personal wealth. That's not true. Throughout the Scriptures God is clear that He wants to prosper people and provide them with abundance. God wants people to be wealthy. God wants you to be wealthy. But God wants the wealth that comes your way to be a tool that you use for His kingdom and your family. He doesn't want the things you own to end up owning you.

God has set up a system where we are all stewards of time, influence, money, relationships, the ability to think and speak and many other things. By stewards I mean that we have the responsibility to manage things that don't belong to us. When we give our lives to Christ, we devote our entire lives to Him. Thus, our time, influence, money, relationships, abilities and every other thing that might come within our sphere of influence all belong to God. He gives those things to us for us to steward for His purposes.

In a sense, money is like every area over which we are stewards. The money that comes our way is often a symbol of our time, influence, relationships, abilities and spheres of influence. Money is power. But it is power that God has put in our lives to use for Him. He has given us money to use as an instrument to serve Him, so we have to steward it wisely. Jesus told a memorable parable to explain this idea.

It will be like a man going on a journey, who called his servants and entrusted his property to them. To one he gave five talents of money, to another two talents, and to another one talent, each according to his ability. Then he went on his journey. The man who had received the five talents went at once and put his money to work and gained five more. So also, the one with the two talents gained two more. But the man who had received the one talent went off, dug a hole in the ground and hid his master's money.

After a long time the master of those servants returned and settled accounts with them. The man who had received the five talents brought the other five. "Master," he said, "you entrusted me with five talents. See, I have gained five more."

His master replied, "Well done, good and faithful servant! You have been faithful with a few things; I will put you in charge of many things. Come and share your master's happiness!"

The man with the two talents also came. "Master," he said, "you entrusted me with two talents; see, I have gained two more."

His master replied, "Well done, good and faithful servant! You have been faithful with a few things; I will put you in charge of many things. Come and share your master's happiness!"

Then the man who had received the one talent came. "Master," he said, "I knew that you are a hard man, harvesting where you have not sown and gathering where you have not scattered seed. So I was afraid and went out and hid your talent in the ground. See, here is what belongs to you."

His master replied, "You wicked, lazy servant! So you knew that I harvest where I have not sown and gather where I have not scattered seed? Well then, you should have put my money on deposit with the bankers, so that when I returned I would have received it back with interest.

"Take the talent from him and give it to the one who has the ten talents. For everyone who has will be given more, and he will have an abundance. Whoever does not have, even what he has will be taken from him. And throw that worthless servant outside, into the darkness, where there will be weeping and gnashing of teeth" (Matt. 25:14-30).

So, in a sense the old cliché is true: The rich get richer and the poor get poorer. Here we see Jesus illustrating the fact that though people begin in different places and situations, the industrious and faithful are rewarded with more opportunity, whereas the lazy and fearful have their opportunities limited. So never be ashamed if you don't have what others have. Instead, be faithful and work with what you've got. Don't make excuses. Don't blame. Don't dig holes. Just be faithful and industrious. God is good. Let His blessing be multiplied in you. If you are faithful in little ways, God will multiply your responsibility and put you in charge of many things. If not, He'll take what little you have and give it to someone else.

When I was growing up on a farm in Indiana, we knew that if we wanted a good crop in the fall it was essential to plant good seed in the springtime. There were other ingredients involved, of course, but if the seed weren't sown properly, the harvest would not be what we wanted.

I quickly learned that all of life is about planting and harvesting. Everything we think is a seed that forms future thoughts and values. Everything we say is a seed that forms future relationships. Everything we do is a seed that establishes our roles with God and with others. Most of the things that happen to us are a result of the seeds that we have sown. Sometimes these seeds sprout quickly; other times they take years before producing a harvest. But they always produce.

Many of our friends are living lives of despair and broken-
ness because of bad seed they planted years ago. Deciding not to
learn to spell is a bad seed. Deciding not to attend school is a bad
seed. Deciding to drive a car too fast is a bad seed. Gossiping to
a coworker about the boss is a bad seed. Watching a bad movie
or looking at something impure on the Internet is a bad seed.
Stealing is a bad seed. Arrogance is a bad seed. And all of these
seeds will produce a bad harvest.

Paul emphasizes this idea in 2 Corinthians 9, where he writes:

Remember this: Whoever sows sparingly will also reap
sparingly, and whoever sows generously will also reap
generously. Each man should give what he has decided
in his heart to give, not reluctantly or under compulsion,
for God loves a cheerful giver. And God is able to make
all grace abound to you, so that in all things at all times,
having all that you need, you will abound in every good
work. As it is written:

"He has scattered abroad his gifts to the poor; his
righteousness endures for ever."

Now he who supplies seed to the sower and bread
for food will also supply and increase your store of seed
and will enlarge the harvest of your righteousness. You
will be made rich in every way so that you can be generous on every occasion, and through us your generosity
will result in thanksgiving to God.

This service that you perform is not only supplying
the needs of God's people but is also overflowing in
many expressions of thanks to God. Because of the service by which you have proved yourselves, men will
praise God for the obedience that accompanies your
confession of the gospel of Christ, and for your generosity in sharing with them and with everyone else (vv. 6-13).

Notice the promises in the eighth verse:

- All grace will abound to you
- In all things
- At all times
- Having all that you need
- You will abound in every good work

Then God promises to increase (multiply) all the seeds you've sown and increase your righteousness. God says He will make you rich so you can be generous toward others. God encourages us to be giving people. But how? First, to the local church. I consider the Old Testament standard of tithing as a plumb line for financial giving to our local church.

As your dad, I obviously want you to start sowing good seed right now. I want you to sow good seed in the way you take care of your bodies, build relationships, learn, grow, think and handle your money. I want your lives to get better and better decade after decade, so as you mature and grow your life can continuously improve.

This is why Jesus said:

Give, and it will be given to you. A good measure, pressed down, shaken together and running over, will be poured into your lap. For with the measure you use, it will be measured to you (Luke 6:38).

It's important for us to realize that we're always sowing seed, we're "giving" with every thought, word and action. Thus, we all need to be very intentional in the way we sow seed, so God can take those seeds and multiply them in our lives.

Every bit of money we receive, no matter the volume of it, is something that we are to steward very carefully. If we plant it according to God's instructions, it will produce a great harvest. In the Old Testament, God commanded His people to give 10 percent of their increase to Him. I feel this is still a good standard for our giving today. We should devote 10 percent of all our income to His work by giving it to Him through the storehouse, which for us is the local church.

The most concise Scripture revealing God's opinion about this is found in Malachi, which reads:

> "Will a man rob God? Yet you rob me. But you ask, 'How do we rob you?' In tithes and offerings. You are under a curse—the whole nation of you—because you are robbing me. Bring the whole tithe [10 percent of our income] into the storehouse [which for us is our local church], that there may be food in my house. Test me in this," says the LORD Almighty, "and see if I will not throw open the floodgates of heaven and pour out so much blessing that you will not have room enough for it. I will prevent pests from devouring your crops, and the vines in your fields will not cast their fruit," says the LORD Almighty. "Then all the nations will call you blessed, for yours will be a delightful land," says the LORD Almighty (vv. 3:8-12).

I am convinced that all believers need to be in healthy life-giving churches and should faithfully tithe there. The tithe indicates our submission of everything in our lives to God, and He promises to bless us for it.

I don't think of tithing as something I just have to do because I am a Christian. I think it's exciting. Tithing is a vital part of my relationship with God. It's one of the ways I trust Him, one of the ways I communicate my love of His work on Earth.

Here is a list of seven reasons why I love to tithe:

1. *It's worship to God.*

Worship is an expression of love, commitment, adoration and respect. When you tithe, you are worshiping God. You are saying to Him that you know He is alive and that you trust Him, that you are living for His good, that you love His kingdom and want His cause furthered. In tithing you are saying that you are committed to His kingdom and that you adore and admire Him. When you give to God, you are looking right at Him and saying you respect everything about Him and want to show it.

2. *It communicates covenant.*

The basis of our relationship with God is the covenant that God established. Some people never discover the power and security of a covenant, and their lives end up shallow, superficial and empty. Covenant relationships make life strong, secure and full. When we tithe, we are demonstrating to God that our covenant with Him is more important than anything else in life. For your mom and me, when we have any income at all in our household, God knows that we will write a check for 10 percent of that income first. So, if He wants to finance something special, He can bless us financially and there is no chance that the money will be redirected or used for something else. We always tithe, no matter what, just like He always forgives, no matter what. It's part of the covenant.

3. *It demonstrates Jesus' work to remove the curse and bless us.*

When a person or family is actively living in covenant with God, it is impossible for the curse of darkness to get very far in their lives. When we tithe, we are expressing our faith in Christ's blessing which often causes our refrigerators to last longer, our teeth to not decay as quickly, our cars to run better. Things work more efficiently; favor rests on us strongly. Our church administrator, who keeps the church records and knows who tithes and who doesn't, says he can see the principle working all the time. He can see the blessing on the lives of those who consistently tithe and the curse on those who don't. Those who don't tithe have to work harder at life, they have to be more diligent, and they don't get the blessings that Malachi talks about. Some of these people complain that they don't have enough seed to tithe from, but . . .

4.   *Tithing provides seeds to multiply.*
Tithing is like exercising or taking a good multiple vitamin. You might not get the benefit today, but there will be a day when you are living well while others are being rushed to the hospital, and you will realize that healthy living is paying off. Tithing is like treating people with respect before they're rich and powerful. It's like investing in Microsoft before Windows. It produces good things in your future.

The story of the talents tells how God will reward us if we are faithful in the small things. I think when we are faithful with $1.00 by tithing $0.10, it's just as significant as tithing $4,000 when $40,000 comes our way. By faithfully tithing on everything we receive, we demonstrate that we're trustworthy and God does, in fact, trust us with more.

When your mom and I were first married, we earned $800 per month. That's right—*per month!* We were so excited to be able to tithe $80 each month. We would write the check on the first of every month after writing the word "seed" on the memo line of the check and asking God to multiply it. He has.

When we started New Life Church, we were so desperate for money that we had to find ways to give. We established New Life as a church that would always sow seed. It has, and because of it, New Life is one of the largest churches in Colorado.

We live on the principle of sowing and reaping. Years ago Oral Roberts said, "Plant a seed to match your need." Tithing is the steady, consistent sowing of seed that always produces harvest. God says we can test Him in this.

5. *It demonstrates our trust toward God and gives God an opportunity to trust us.*

When we have little, it's tempting to keep it all for ourselves. Our human reasoning tells us that we'd better protect what we have and not let any of it get away. But God wants us to trust Him in spite of our circumstances. He wants us to believe that He will take care of us. If we do, and if He can see that we trust Him, then He will trust us with more of His work, His favor and His riches.

6. *It's a tangible way to demonstrate what we believe.*

Too often people say they believe certain things about God, but don't do anything to reflect that. This is the mark of a fool. When we truly believe something, it should impact what we do. Our actions should validate our words. When they do, both people and God can trust us. So when we tithe, it demonstrates that we really believe what we say we believe and gives God the opportunity to confirm His reality in our lives.

7. *It involves us in God's purpose.*

Local churches are the number one place God has chosen to disciple His people. And local churches are the number one source of funding for missions and other special ministry projects. At New Life Church alone, we give about $2,000,000 every year to people and projects outside our church to advance God's kingdom. None of us alone could do that, but because the church is our storehouse, it becomes an armory where we build up cumulative strength and are able to advance with great force. Then, when the storehouses of the world—the local churches—partner with servant ministries that are supported by offerings, the selling of products, etc., the force is incredible. But if people neglect their local churches, God's purpose is hindered. I want to faithfully be a participant in His perfect will, so I tithe to a church that supports servant ministries from the storehouse.

Okay, okay, okay! I can hear you saying, "Dad, I'm convinced! I believe it. But how do I do it? What systems do I use to give? How do I know where to give? How do I become rich toward God?"

Remember these six things:

1. *Give according to your income.*

The idea is in Deuteronomy 16:17, where the Bible says: "Each of you must bring a gift in proportion to the way the LORD you God has blessed you." At our house, we tithe our personal income, which means everything that comes into our household. We tithe all gifts and finances that come our way through any means. If we owned a business, we would tithe the profits of the business. This is a great system because God blesses us in order to funnel things into His kingdom. He knows that we will do it, and He trusts us. Actually, tithing brings us greater joy than anything else we do with our income.

2. *Give without ostentation.*

Matthew 6 has a lot to say about the heart of a giver in God's kingdom. The bottom line, though, is to give innocently. Don't give based on whether or not someone will put a plaque up in your name. Actually, don't allow them to do that. If they insist on a plaque, put someone else's name on it. Never be motivated to give in order to receive praises from men or a position on a board or anything like that. Give to God, and let men settle their own hearts. And don't give based on the attention you receive from a ministry. The purpose of those ministries is to minister, not to take care of you. Unfortunately, too many ministries waste money to coddle people into giving to good causes. Shame on those who respond to that type of thing and on those who expect it. Give to God, and never let your heart become so proud that you expect recognition for your giving.

Christy and Marcus, did you know that the top giver at New Life Church is a man I've never met? He gives significant amounts in accordance with his income, but he gives it like everyone else. He's never tried to contact me, be in control of any of the church's decisions or expected special attention. He's obviously a man of God.

Unfortunately, some churches actually monitor giving and do special things for major donors. I don't think this encourages godliness among the givers. People are often so carnal that they give more in order to receive special recognition. Don't allow your hearts to be trapped into this trick. Just tithe and be respectful to people, and don't give in response to special attention.

3. *Give freely, with a cheerful heart.*
Here is my policy: If they ask too strongly, I don't give. If they try to manipulate my emotions, I don't give. If they try to manipulate my relationship with God by suggesting that God will like me more if I give, I don't give. I give because I am a Christian, and I direct my giving to my local storehouse which I trust will use a portion of the funds for servant ministries and special projects. I give it cheerfully, not because I'm asked to or because I've been talked into it, but because I'm a Christian.

4. *Give with simplicity.*
How do I give $100,000 to a church? Is there some special protocol for huge gifts? No. Just put your check in the offering plate like everyone else. Don't make a big deal of it.

5. *Give with regularity.*

How often should I give? As often as I am paid or receive any income. I know people who try to tithe annually so they can use the money for more income throughout the year. This usually doesn't work, and very often their income does not increase the way they had projected it. Often these folks end up not tithing at all because God doesn't bless them as strongly. Others miss the point by trying to tithe things, which is a kind thought, but not to the point.

Tithing is simple, not complicated. Every time you receive any money, write a tithe check and take it to church the next weekend or send it to the church. Then, the church can plan and budget knowing that you don't have to be talked into giving.

6. *Give with a cheerful heart.*

As I mentioned earlier, the greatest joy I have in my finances is in giving to my local church and from time to time giving offerings to others who are doing a good work. I never give my tithe to anyone other than our local church, but I do give special offerings to others. The joy that comes into our lives realizing the blessing that this brings is incredible, and I know, without a doubt, that this is the way to be rich toward God.

I am writing about expressing your loving relationship with God through the things you think, say and do. If the world were a perfect place, the principles I have outlined in this letter would work universally for everyone without exception. But since we are on Earth, there will always be persecution. There will always be an enemy fighting to keep you from faithfulness toward God. So give no matter what. Exercise these core principles regardless of the consequence. You might receive your reward in heaven rather than here on Earth. The bottom line is that we believe and act in obedience because of Christ's faithfulness, not for personal gain. And when you plant positive seeds, it does help for a more positive future—sooner or later!

So, Christy and Marcus, I think you have the idea. God wants to bless you financially, but if you don't understand His will and plan, you may end up with money here on Earth but find yourself without treasure in heaven. The solution: Be rich toward God. Tithe, plan and be faithful in the small things so He can trust you with greater things. With this plan, you may find yourself wealthy on Earth and in heaven.

I love you so much. God bless you!

I love being your dad,

REFLECTION AND DISCUSSION

1. How do you become rich toward God?
2. Explain how seeds produce a harvest.
3. What does it mean to be a steward of something?
4. Does tithing have more to do with money or with our hearts toward God? How do you know?

SEEK THE KINGDOM OF GOD

February 26

Dear Christy and Marcus,

It's a beautiful Monday afternoon, and I've spent most of it thinking about how to write this next letter to you. I'm really excited about what I am getting ready to tell you, because I know if you understand this idea, it will strengthen you every day of your lives.

As you go through life, you'll be constantly reminded that human beings are desperately searching for an explanation of why things are the way they are. If God is good, why is there evil? If prayer works, why are there sick people? Is a spiritual life actually tangible? Why are there so many opinions? How do we find out how to live the right way?

These are all good questions, but most of these questions would be solved by grasping a few basic biblical ideas that make life work. All of these letters I've been writing you have been about these ideas, but today I'm going to try to explain the most important one. Everything I've written to you boils down to one powerful idea: seeking the kingdom of God.

Jesus says to His disciples in Luke 12,

Therefore I tell you, do not worry about your life, what you will eat; or about your body, what you will wear. Life is more than food, and the body more than clothes. Consider the ravens: They do not sow or reap, they have no storeroom or barn; yet God feeds them. And how much more valuable you are than birds! Who of you by worrying can add a single hour to his life? Since you cannot do this very little thing, why do you worry about the rest?

Consider how the lilies grow. They do not labor or spin. Yet I tell you, not even Solomon in all his splendor was dressed like one of these. If that is how God clothes the grass of the field, which is here today, and tomorrow is thrown into the fire, how much more will he clothe you, O you of little faith! And do not set your heart on what you will eat or drink; do not worry about it. For the pagan world runs after all such things, and your Father knows that you need them. *But seek his kingdom, and these things will be given to you as well.*

Do not be afraid, little flock, for your Father has been pleased to give you the kingdom. Sell your possessions and give to the poor. Provide purses for yourselves that will not wear out, a treasure in heaven that will not be exhausted, where no thief comes near and no moth destroys. For where your treasure is, there your heart will be also (vv. 22-34, emphasis added).

As I've been explaining to you throughout these letters, it's very important that you understand how much God wants to take care of you. That's why He shares the secrets of life with you. In this passage, He tells how much He loves you and that the solution to your needs is not seeking those things, but seeking His Kingdom.

This is the great news of Jesus' message. It's what makes the gospel good news. We are valuable to God. No matter what we've done He loves us, wants us near Him and longs for us to live with Him and serve Him. He longs to meet our needs.

But if this is true, why do so many people live in great need? Why do they struggle from month to month acquiring things, but never finding lasting satisfaction? It's because they neglect to seek God's Kingdom. Jesus' words in Luke 12 couldn't be clearer: If we seek the kingdom of God, what we need will be provided for us. And that's the next principle for successful living I want to highlight for you:

SEEK THE KINGDOM OF GOD.

So what is the kingdom of God? The easiest way to understand the meaning of "kingdom" is to unpack the two syllables: it's the *dominion* of a *king*. The kingdom of God is the place where King Jesus has full dominion. When we seek first His Kingdom, we're seeking the place where Jesus' will is fully manifested.

God wants His will done on Earth, which is why we're commanded to pray: "Your kingdom come, your will be done on earth as it is in heaven" (Matt. 6:10). In heaven, God's perfect will is completely manifested. There are no hospitals because no one is sick. No one is overweight or anorexic; no one is angry or apathetic. There are no betrayals, no pain, no tears of sorrow. Everything is perfect. Everyone feels good; everyone is happy and fulfilled; people are happy and no one ever gets their feelings hurt.

In heaven, you can go swimming and never get tired. In heaven you can travel as fast as you like and never slow down. In heaven you can love unconditionally and never worry about being misunderstood. There is no jealousy, murder, strife or heartbreak.

Heaven is better than Earth. It's a great place. And we call it the kingdom of heaven or the kingdom of God because it's under the lordship of Jesus. It's where God has full dominion. In heaven, there is no violation of His will. That's why:

> Jesus went through all the towns and villages, teaching in their synagogues, preaching the good news of the kingdom and healing every disease and sickness (Matt. 9:35).

It's normal on Earth for people to be sick, but when God's kingdom is manifested around people, they get healed.

When Jesus was commissioning His disciples to teach, He said,

> As you go, preach this message; "The kingdom of heaven is near." Heal the sick, raise the dead, cleanse those who have leprosy, drive out demons. Freely you have received, freely give (Matt. 10:7-8).

He wanted His disciples to explain that God's kingdom is available, and to prove it they were going to show people what happens in God's kingdom: People are physically strong, people are alive, people are clean, people are healthy—and it's all free.

The reception of His kingdom in this evil world is like the invasion of good into evil. It's a war, which is why Jesus said: "The kingdom of heaven has been forcefully advancing, and forceful men lay hold of it" (Matt. 11:12). This is a violent invasion of one supreme Ruler over an inferior one, and it requires forceful people to obtain it. That's why we must seek the kingdom of God—it's a powerful, mysterious, supernatural phenomenon, and it works.

Before we know Christ, our lives are devoted to earthly things. But when the kingdom of heaven takes hold of our lives, a clash takes place because heaven and Earth are very different. Heaven is full of peace; Earth is filled with war. Heaven is for healing; Earth harbors destruction. Heaven is love; Earth is dominated by hate. When God's kingdom invades Earth through prayer, the conflict is evident. It's a war.

When we seek the kingdom of heaven, we are asking God to send a slice of heaven to Earth. He does this through His Holy Spirit. When we accept Jesus as Lord and Savior, the Holy Spirit actually comes into our lives; our hearts receive a deposit of God's kingdom.

I can hear you saying right now: "Come on, Dad. Tell us straight. Why are things the way they are? We believe that God is good, but why is life hard for so many people?"

Life can be hard because God's kingdom is not always the dominant force in people's lives. You see, there are four powerful forces that influence the world:

- The will of God
- The power of darkness and the devil
- The self-will of people (i.e., their sinful nature)
- The natural laws governing our physical world

Everything that happens to you involves at least one of these things, though the four forces are probably always influencing you simultaneously in some way. God's will is for His Kingdom to rule and for people to be free, but Satan and the forces of darkness are a reality and have to be dealt with in people's lives. Additionally, humankind has selfishness and sensuality dominating much of their lives, so dealing with sin is a constant battle. On top of all that, the natural laws created by God have dominant control over our physical environment.

Earth is not heaven. People here are sick (natural law), tormented (forces of darkness) and selfish (sinful nature). God wants to liberate them by allowing them into another kingdom—His kingdom, the kingdom of God.

Some will tell you that since God is sovereign, everything that happens to every person on Earth does so according to His perfect will. If this were true then all poverty, sickness, depravity, hurt and suffering would be God's doing—His plan. But God's sovereignty as exercised on Earth means that His overall, long-term plan for mankind will be fulfilled. He sovereignly ensures that His promises are kept and His Word enforced. That's why the context of the five New Testament references to God's Sovereignty centers around times of suffering and negative situations. In the midst of all the heartache of living in a fallen world, God reminds His people that the last word is still His (see Luke 2:29; Acts 4:24; 2 Pet. 2:1; Jude 4; Rev. 6:10)!

The mysterious courses of your lives are for the purpose of fulfilling God's plan, which *will* be completed. Because of your old sin nature and the influence of darkness in the Earth, none of us is capable of seeking God or seeking His kingdom on our own. We need God. And He is sovereignly reaching into you and calling you to Himself. But you must choose whether or not to respond. I want to encourage you to seek His kingdom and obey His Spirit in order to ensure your participation in the demonstration of His kingdom on Earth. Don't ignore His call and go your own way.

The Bible is the book that God sent to us to illustrate how people interact with God and His kingdom. Throughout Scripture God offers us promises, gives us commandments, responds to prayer, illustrates His work among people and nations and communicates the benefits of obedience and the consequences of disobedience. God set up Earth as a place where we could make choices about Him and ourselves so that He would have people in heaven that love and worship him freely. We have a part to play, a choice to make: Will we seek His Kingdom or not?

Sin is missing God's plan for our lives. It's going our own way. It's doing what we want to do. It's a violation of God's will, and it prevails in many people's lives. The Bible's first reference to sin is in Genesis 4, where it says:

> If you do what is right, will you not be accepted? But if you do not do what is right, sin is crouching at your door; it desires to have you, but you must master it (v. 7).

There are lots of lists of sins in the Bible. Probably the most famous one in the New Testament is in Galatians 5, where Paul writes:

> The acts of the sinful nature are obvious; sexual immorality, impurity and debauchery; idolatry and witchcraft; hatred, discord, jealousy, fits of rage, selfish ambition, dissensions, factions and envy; drunkenness, orgies, and the like. I warn you, as I did before, that those who live like this will not inherit the kingdom of God (vv. 19-21).

Sin comes from two sources. The first place is the devil and his demons. There is a devil, Satan, and he is alive on the earth right now. In John 10, Jesus referred to him as the thief when He said, "The thief comes only to steal and kill and destroy; I [Jesus] have come that they may have life, and have it to the full" (v. 10).

The devil and his demons steal, kill and destroy all the time. They whisper to people. They plant seeds of ungodly thoughts. They do everything in their power to get a person off track. They tempt, seduce and, if they can, actually occupy people's bodies so they can directly influence their thoughts and actions. That's why, in the Gospels, you read so often about Jesus driving demons out of people. He wants people to be free to experience the kingdom of God through His lordship.

The second source of sin is our own sinful nature. When the Bible speaks of the sinful nature, it's talking about the desire for independence from God that resides within every person. Everyone is born with a bent toward sin, and this must be dealt with through learning the Scriptures and relying on the power of the Holy Spirit. This sinful nature has to be put to death. If it's not, it will seek to take over and destroy a person's life. Romans 7 says,

> For when we were controlled by the sinful nature, the sinful passions aroused by the law were at work in our bodies, so that we bore fruit for death (v. 5).

Paul goes on to highlight how powerful our sinful tendencies are:

> I know that nothing good lives in me, that is, in my sinful nature. For I have the desire to do what is good, but I cannot carry it out (v. 18).

So we must struggle against our sinful nature and make ourselves respond to the Holy Spirit instead of temptation.

The fourth force is natural law. Natural law is the reason we wear seat belts, drive the speed limit and have fire extinguishers in public places. Natural law is a force that is always at work in the world. It is a reality that God set up to rule a great deal of our existence. If you intentionally jumped out of an airplane without a parachute and died, it would be foolish for people to say that it was the will of God or that the devil did it. You would have died as a consequence of a natural law—in that case gravity.

God created, sustains and sometimes may suspend or alter these three natural forces. As I have already said, when God manifests His power and dominion, we experience an inbreaking of the kingdom of God. When God exercises His will over demons, we call that *deliverance* from demonic bondage. When God exercises His will over our rebellious sinful nature, we call that being *Spirit filled* or Spirit controlled. When God supernaturally overrides natural law, we call that a *miracle*. And all of these things happen regularly when we seek His kingdom.

How do we seek His kingdom? Through prayer? Yes. Through Bible study? No doubt. And also by living according to His perfect will. When we resist sin and keep our hearts and lives clean before the Lord, we're seeking His kingdom.

The kingdom of God is the manifestation of His power in the midst of powerlessness. It takes no supernatural power for people to lie, to cheat, to steal, to break the law, to hate people and to be wicked. It takes the power of God, though, for people to be honest, to give, to obey, to love and to be kind. In the Sermon on the Mount, Jesus said: "Blessed are the poor in spirit, for theirs is the kingdom of heaven" (Matt. 5:3). When people are arrogant, self-consumed and high-minded, they will not be able to enjoy, proclaim or advance the kingdom of heaven. But God wants people to enjoy the benefits of His kingdom and to be able to escape the bondages of their sinful nature and sinful society. That's why we want to communicate the gospel. The message that we preach is that in the coming of Jesus, the kingdom of heaven has come to the earth. In Matthew 10:7, Jesus commands His followers: "As you go, preach this message: 'The kingdom of heaven is near.'"

I mentioned earlier that for most people (even Christians) the kingdom of heaven is a mystery, but it doesn't have to be. Of course, we can't scientifically explain how it works or plot it on a graph, but we can understand that if we trust God and seek

His kingdom, He will be faithful to us. Jesus once told His disciples:

> The knowledge of the secrets of the kingdom of heaven has been given to you, but not to them. Whoever has will be given more, and he will have an abundance. Whoever does not have, even what he has will be taken from him (Matt. 13:11-12).

The message for us here is that the kingdom of heaven has been given to us too, and if we humble ourselves and seek the kingdom of heaven, we will obtain it.

In this same conversation, Jesus described those who go through life without the kingdom of heaven operating in their lives. He said:

> Though seeing, they do not see; though hearing, they do not hear or understand. In them is fulfilled the prophecy of Isaiah: "You will be ever hearing but never understanding; you will be ever seeing but never perceiving. For this people's heart has become calloused; they hardly hear with their ears, and they have closed their eyes. Otherwise they might see with their eyes, hear with their ears, understand with their hearts and turn, and I would heal them" (vv. 13-15).

But to His followers like you, He gives hope:

> But blessed are your eyes because they see, and your ears because they hear. For I tell you the truth, many prophets and righteous men longed to see what you see but did not see it, and to hear what you hear but did not hear it (vv. 16-17).

Some people get confused about the idea of the kingdom of heaven being on Earth because bad things still happen. They assume that since God is sovereign—which He is—everything that happens on Earth must be His will. That's just not true. Everything that happens in His kingdom must be His will, but things do happen outside His kingdom that are not His will.

That's why it's extremely valuable to us to seek His kingdom. He rewards us by taking care of us. He says the kingdom of heaven is like a treasure hidden in a field or a rare jewel—it's precious and valuable. Imagine the thing that most excites you, that you're willing to work for tirelessly until you get it. That's what the kingdom of heaven is like. It's worth risking our very lives to find and obtain it.

But the kingdom of heaven is worth seeking for another reason too: We don't want to be part of the group that misses it. (Remember the letter about fearing God?) Jesus spoke about the severity of the kingdom of heaven when He said,

> The kingdom of heaven is like a net that was let down into the lake and caught all kinds of fish. When it was full, the fishermen pulled it up on the shore. Then they sat down and collected the good fish in baskets, but threw the bad away. This is how it will be at the end of the age. The angels will come and separate the wicked from the righteous and throw them into the fiery furnace, where there will be weeping and gnashing of teeth (Matt. 13:47-50).

God doesn't want anyone to miss His kingdom. He says in 2 Peter 3 that He is "not wanting anyone to perish, but everyone to come to repentance" (v. 9). The earth is full of disobedience, and because of it, many people never find the Kingdom. But the kingdom of heaven is available to all who seek it humbly.

To demonstrate the powerful effects of the kingdom of God, Jesus said in Luke 13, "[The kingdom of God] is like yeast that a woman took and mixed into a large amount of flour until it worked all through the dough" (v. 21). A little bit of Kingdom makes a difference in all of life. That's why we pray as He taught us: "Your kingdom come, your will be done on earth as it is in heaven" (Matt. 6:10). We want His lordship manifest to be both in our lives and in the lives of people all over the earth.

Think about this. Talk about it with your friends. Search the Scriptures, and seek God's kingdom, and let His miracles and supernatural control dominate every area of your life. Trust Him, and His blessings will flow in power.

I love being your dad,

REFLECTION AND DISCUSSION

1. What does it mean to seek the kingdom of God?
2. When we pray for God's kingdom to come, what are we praying for?
3. Can you explain why some people have hard lives? What forces are at work to make our lives good or bad? How can we respond to those forces?
4. Why do you think God permits things to happen that are not His will?

BE DRESSED AND READY TO SERVE GOD

February 27

Dear Christy and Marcus,

There is a story in today's paper about two teenage boys accused of killing their professor at Dartmouth College. One of the boys, a sharp-looking young man, is shown with handcuffs on his wrists which are in turn chained to his waist. His ankles are shackled, forcing him to shuffle along between the two officers who flank him on each side.

Also in the paper is a story about a young man in Southern California who intentionally drove his car into a group of people yesterday evening, killing four of them. Witnesses say he jumped out of the car afterwards and was yelling, "I am the death angel!" as he flailed around swinging at people until the police came and subdued him.

What a waste. All of these young men had opportunities to excel. Two were established at a premier university, and one was related to key people in Hollywood. But they squandered their potential. No doubt we are going to hear all about the psychological difficulties these young men faced, making it seem as if it were inevitable that they would commit these crimes. That's misleading and beside the point. There are people all over the world who have difficulties and still find ways to make good decisions with their lives. Harsh circumstances don't produce bad people. Bad decisions do.

Christy and Marcus, I want you to think clearly about these kinds of situations. In both accounts we see wasted lives, wasted investment by parents and wasted opportunities in that we're not going to be able to enjoy the benefit we could have had from these young people. Why? Because they chose to live for themselves, to follow their worst impulses and to make others suffer. The book of Proverbs says that wisdom and folly call out to each of us. We hear both voices wooing us, and we have to choose between them. It's up to us to make the right choice. No one can do it for us, and if we make the wrong choice, no one is to blame except us.

The reason I love writing you about Jesus' teaching from Luke 12 is that everything He says boils down to making good, godly choices. Wisely choose to live as if there are no secrets. Decide to fear God, not people. Believe that God values you and that you can honor Him in public. Willfully open yourself up to the ministry of the Holy Spirit. Be strong and stable under pressure, make sound decisions with your money, and confidently seek His kingdom every day. If you believe these principles and learn to do them, your lives will be successful, contented and meaningful.

But you have to be ready to do it. You always need to be prepared to make good choices. Sometimes, people feel like it's okay to take a break from seeking God. If they've been living well for a while, they'll convince themselves that they can ease off, that maybe they don't really need to be in church or spend much time in prayer. But this is dangerous thinking. We need to stay steady, consistently seeking God's kingdom.

In Luke 12:35-48, Jesus says,

Be dressed ready for service and keep your lamps burning, like men waiting for their master to return from a wedding banquet, so that when he comes and knocks they can immediately open the door for him. It will be good for those servants whose master finds them watching when he comes. I tell you the truth, he will dress himself to serve, will have them recline at the table and will come and wait on them. It will be good for those servants whose master finds them ready, even if he comes in the second or third watch of the night. But understand this: If the owner of the house had known at what hour the thief was coming, he would not have let his house be broken into. You also must be ready, because the Son of Man will come at an hour when you do not expect him.

Peter asked, "Lord, are you telling this parable to us, or to everyone?"

The Lord answered, "Who then is the faithful and wise manager, whom the master puts in charge of his servants to give them their food allowance at the proper time? It will be good for that servant whom the master finds doing so when he returns. I tell you the truth, he will put him in charge of all his possessions. But suppose the servant says to himself, 'My master is taking a long time in coming,' and he then begins to beat the menservants and maidservants and to eat and drink and get drunk. The master of that servant will come on a day when he does not expect him and at an hour he is not aware of. He will cut him to pieces and assign him a place with the unbelievers.

"That servant who knows his master's will and does not get ready or does not do what his master wants will be beaten with many blows. But the one who does not know and does things deserving punishment will be beaten with few blows. From everyone who has been given much, much will be demanded; and from the one who has been entrusted with much, much more will be asked."

Have you ever gone somewhere with the wrong clothes on? I have, and I hate it. Or have you ever had someone show up at our house right after you woke up, and you have to open the door and talk with them before you can get dressed or do anything with your hair, and you feel stuck and a little embarrassed?

Jesus wants us to always be "dressed." He doesn't want us to be caught off guard. He wants us prepared to work with Him and His kingdom. And this is the next principle of successful living that I want to share with you:

BE DRESSED AND READY TO SERVE GOD.

So how do we get dressed to serve him? And what do we wear? The answer is the subject of my last letter: Seek God's kingdom. If we seek the kingdom of God, God will clothe us—both physically and spiritually. If we seek Him, He will provide for our needs, and more importantly, He will clothe us in His attributes. Check out these Scriptures:

If that is how God clothes the grass of the field, which is here today and tomorrow is thrown into the fire, will he not much more clothe you, O you of little faith? So do not worry, saying, "What shall we eat?" or "What shall we drink?" or "What shall we wear?" For the pagans run after all these things, and your heavenly Father knows that you need them. But seek first his kingdom and his righteousness, and all these things will be given to you as well. Therefore do not worry about tomorrow, for tomorrow will worry about itself. Each day has enough trouble of its own (Matt. 6:30-34).

Clothe yourselves with the Lord Jesus Christ, and do not think about how to gratify the desires of the sinful nature (Rom. 13:14).

Therefore, as God's chosen people, holy and dearly loved, clothe yourselves with compassion, kindness, humility, gentleness and patience. Bear with each other and forgive whatever grievances you may have against one another. Forgive as the Lord forgave you. And over all these virtues put on love, which binds them all together in prefect unity (Col. 3:12-14).

Young men, in the same way be submissive to those who are older. All of you, clothe yourselves with humility toward one another, because, "God opposes the proud but gives grace to the humble." Humble yourselves, therefore, under God's mighty hand, that he may lift you up in due time. Cast all your anxiety on him because he cares for you. Be self-controlled and alert. Your enemy the devil prowls around like a roaring lion looking for someone to devour. Resist him, standing firm in the faith, because you know that your brothers throughout the world are undergoing the same kind of sufferings (1 Pet. 5:5-9).

Can we do this? Can we actually put on compassion like we put on pants? Can we wear kindness like we wear a shirt? Can we be seen in humility the way we're seen in a jacket? Yes, we can. We clothe ourselves every time we seek the Kingdom.

Christy and Marcus, there are lots of wonderful biblical ideas that will keep you dressed and ready to serve God. Today I just want to write to you about three of them which I believe are fundamentally important.

1. *Remember sowing and reaping.*

As I wrote in another letter to you, everything you think, say and do is a seed that will influence your future. There is real power in our thoughts to shape our lives. That's why a snowboarder can lie in bed and think about flowing from edge to edge, jump to jump, and then the next day he is better than he was before. Or a basketball player can visualize himself making shot after shot, and the thoughts of playing well actually help him on the court.

Paul was a strong believer in the power of our thoughts to determine our future. He wrote:

> The mind of sinful man is death, but the mind controlled by the Spirit is life and peace; the sinful mind is hostile to God. It does not submit to God's law, nor can it do so (Rom. 8:6-8).

The way we think will determine the road ahead. Every thought is a seed, so we prepare ourselves for His work by controlling the things we think about. The Bible tells us how to discipline our thoughts when it says:

> Do not think of yourself more highly than you ought, but rather think of yourself with sober judgment, in accordance with the measure of faith God has given you (Rom. 12:3).

Another warning is found in 1 Corinthians 10:12, where Paul writes: "So, if you think you are standing firm, be careful that you don't fall!"

I have two favorite verses on this subject. The first is Philippians 4:8, which says:

Finally, brothers, whatever is true, whatever is noble, whatever is right, whatever is pure, whatever is lovely, whatever is admirable—if anything is excellent or praiseworthy—think about such things.

The other is Romans 12:2, where Paul writes:

Do not conform any longer to the pattern of this world, but be transformed by the renewing of your mind. Then you will be able to test and approve what God's will is— his good, pleasing and perfect will.

It's right there: Fulfilling God's primary will for our lives is either prospered or hindered by how we think.

When I travel, I like to take others along with me so we can take time in the morning for "manna." Manna, for me, is a time to read the Scriptures and talk about the ideas with another person. Every time I do this I learn something, and it's fun. I let my thoughts be influenced by the ideas in the Scriptures, and I'm strengthened by those ideas. Why do I do this? Because the difference between a police officer and a thief is the thoughts they think. The difference between Joseph Stalin, who murdered between 20 and 40 million of his own citizens, and Mother Teresa, who brought hope and blessing to millions around the world, was their thoughts. I want my thoughts to be filled with hope, insight and trust in God.

Controlling our thoughts flows right into the next point: controlling our words. God created the heavens and the earth by speaking. God reveals Himself by speaking. We express our thoughts by speaking. Words are powerful and important. They mean something, and they have the power to create wonderful things or horribly destructive things. Jesus said in Matthew 12:37: "For by your words you will be acquitted, and by your words you will be condemned." In explaining the importance of His words, Jesus said in Matthew 24:35: "Heaven and earth will pass away, but my words will never pass away." What God says matters. And what you say matters too.

Proverbs 15:4 says: "The tongue that brings healing is a tree of life, but a deceitful tongue crushes the spirit." Christy and Marcus, with your words you can cause people to be great or you can pollute them and ruin their lives. With your words you can create life in people's hearts and minds or you can create death and destruction. Jesus says that His ministry was validated by the words He spoke: "For the one whom God has sent speaks the words of God, for God gives the Spirit without limit" (John 3:34). The same is true with us. Our words identify who sent us.

In 1 Corinthians 2 Paul says that words are of utmost importance in communicating truth. He writes,

> This is what we speak, not in words taught us by human wisdom but in words taught by the Spirit, expressing spiritual truths in spiritual words (v. 13).

This is why James insisted that we control our speech when he said in James 3:

> Likewise the tongue is a small part of the body, but it makes great boasts. Consider what a great forest is set on fire by a small spark. The tongue also is a fire, a world of evil among the parts of the body. It corrupts the whole person, sets the whole course of his life on fire, and is itself set on fire by hell (vv. 5-6).

So everything we say is also a seed that will produce a harvest.

What we think flows into what we speak, which in turn leads to what we do. This is a powerful principle to learn, because it teaches us to sow seed specifically into the areas in which we want to reap a harvest. Sow financial seeds to reap financial harvest; sow seeds of love to reap a harvest of acceptance. Sow seeds of study to reap a harvest of being able to teach others. Sow seeds of life to reap a harvest of joy. Everything we do, whether making a phone call, sending a card, helping someone in need, watching a movie or reading a book is a seed that creates and produces a harvest. If we sow good seed, we'll always be dressed and ready.

2.   *Stay connected with the Body of Christ.*

I know sometimes the two of you hesitate about going to Sunday service or attending one of the church meetings, but I want to try to explain the great miracle of the Body of Christ.

Just as your physical body is made up of billions of cells that take care of one another, so the church is a variety of people who take care of one another. Your body has different members (eyes, ears, hair, tongue, fingers, etc.) that when connected properly allow you to function well. Likewise, the church is a group of people that, when connected, make things work well for everyone. The church building or service really isn't the issue; the issue is connecting with the church body in a healthy, life-giving way. This is what makes life worth living. When we are well connected in our church, we all become more successful. Everyone has strong areas and weak areas in his or her lives. In the church, we want to connect with those who have strength where we are weak, so they can coach us, so our weaknesses don't end up defining our lives. In the same way, we need to use our strengths to serve people who are weak, so we can coach them in being successful in an area of their lives where they might otherwise fail.

In our church body, there are people who know how to study, learn, pray, have a great marriage, make investments, travel, scuba dive, sky dive and buy cars. There are also people in our church body who don't have a clue how to do some of these things. If these people just sit side by side on a Sunday morning and never meet, they can still be individually promoted by their personal strengths, but their weaknesses will always cause trouble for them. But if they are connected to one another in the church, their strengths can strengthen others, their weaknesses can be minimized, and everyone can have greater success.

This is why the local church is so important. It's the place where we connect and so encourage one another to enjoy the lives that the Lord plans for us. If we are connected to the body in a healthy way, there is no reason for any of us to fail. If the body works the way it should, with long-term healthy relationships, no one in the body ever needs to be homeless, without medical care or without food and shelter. When you are connected in the body, you are safe, protected and stable.

3. *Understand biblical authority.*

Now, don't put this letter down right here and turn away! I think this principle is one of the most wonderful and empowering principles in all of life. Those who grab on to this principle and apply it to their lives trigger many things that make it possible for material and spiritual things to be added to their lives in a significant way. Once we understand how God has set up Earth, the door is opened for us to operate within His systems of authority with honor and, in turn, to have a greater likelihood of receiving His blessings.

God arranged four systems of authority on the earth: the family, the church, the workplace and civic government. As we seek the kingdom of God, we have to understand that it works within these four structures. If we align our lives within these structures, His blessing can flow.

The Family

Our society is waging war against the family right now, and we are paying a heavy price for it. You might say that you don't agree with the principles of the family as God designed it, but you have to understand that these are the institutions God set up to bless people, and that if we use them wisely they will be a blessing to everyone.

Ephesians 5:22-30 says:

> Wives, submit to your husbands as to the Lord. For the husband is the head of the wife as Christ is the head of the church, his body, of which he is the Savior. Now as the church submits to Christ, so also wives should submit to their husbands in everything. Husbands, love your wives, just as Christ loved the church and gave himself up for her to make her holy, cleansing her by the washing with water through the word. . . . In this same way, husbands ought to love their wives as their own bodies. He who loves his wife loves himself. After all, no one ever hated his own body, but he feeds and cares for it, just as Christ does the church—for we are members of his body.

Now, Christy and Marcus, you will have friends, professors, teachers and TV personalities tell you that the passage above is not true. But they don't know. They are guessing. Because of people not liking this material, we have a 70 percent divorce rate here in Colorado Springs, and both of you have way too many friends whose parents have gone their own way and split the family. But there is no reason to lose our families. These biblical ideas can be applied with success. Families have done it for centuries. We're doing it right now.

We also believe what the Bible says about the relationship between parents and children. Ephesians 6:1-3:

> Children, obey your parents in the Lord, for this is right. "Honor your father and mother"—which is the first commandment with a promise—"that it may go well with you and that you may enjoy long life on the earth."

This is simple stuff: God is telling young men and women that if they honor their parents, things will go well for them. It's no mystery. It's easy. Once we understand our position in our family as God intended it, it's simple to live within these structures.

The Church

The church is not just a place of inspiration; it's a place of instruction. In the church, there are men and women appointed to be our life coaches. Our church leaders, our small-group leaders, Sunday School teachers and youth pastors are all devoted to the success of those they are teaching.

First Timothy 5 says:

> The elders who direct the affairs of the church well are worthy of double honor, especially those whose work is preaching and teaching (v. 17).

We need to be supremely respectful of those who are directly over us. God has placed them there: Our role is to honor them, listen to them and treat them with respect.

Don't ever fall into the trap of becoming cynical about your teachers. If you don't agree with everything they say or have problems with their style, that's fine, but remember that as long as they are in positions of authority over you, your role is to honor them. God will bless you if you maintain innocence and keep yourself free of judging others. If you hear your friends starting to make fun of Christian leaders, just quietly dismiss yourself from the conversation or find ways to turn criticism into compliments.

When I was a youth pastor working for brother Roy Stockstill at Bethany World Prayer Center, I always made a point of carrying around a notebook and pen. I didn't make a big show of it, but whenever we were in a scheduled meeting, I'd take notes on everything he said. If we were working or even just talking casually and entered into an impromptu meeting, I'd pull out the notebook and carefully highlight his main points. Not only did this help me to do my job well, but it also communicated to brother Stockstill and to God that I knew who was in charge, and I wanted to respectfully honor God's chosen leadership.

The Workplace

The workplace is another area of God's established authority that people have overcomplicated. Today, too many people spend too much time thinking about their rights as workers and worrying about whether they are being treated with respect. Or they try to work as little as possible and make sure that their personal free time is not infringed upon.

You will probably have a number of jobs in your lifetime, and you may work for lots of different types of bosses or be a boss over lots of different types of people. Some will be fair and honest, others may not. No matter what your situation, your role is to work as unto God, with respect, dignity and integrity.

In Colossians 3, Paul writes:

Slaves, obey your earthly masters in everything; and do it, not only when their eye is on you and to win their favor, but with sincerity of heart and reverence for the Lord. Whatever you do, work at it with all your heart, as working for the Lord, not for men, since you know that you will receive an inheritance from the Lord as a reward. It is the Lord Christ you are serving (vv. 22-24).

Now, in Paul's day, slaves were often treated much like workers are treated today—with a certain amount of care and respect. They were more like lifelong servants than your traditional notion of a slave. So this can apply to us today in how we are to do our jobs. We don't work for temporary earthly rewards. We seek God's kingdom even in our jobs, knowing that He holds the promise of the best rewards. He is our Boss. He writes our paychecks. We work for Him.

The secret to honoring God's authority in the workplace is to maintain a consistent, godly, innocent perspective, no matter what the circumstance. Again, you can choose the condition of your heart in any situation. In 1 Corinthians 4, Paul writes:

We work hard with our own hands. When we are cursed, we bless; when we are persecuted, we endure it; when we are slandered, we answer kindly (vv. 12-13).

Paul knew that he was working as unto God. He was respectful, hardworking and innocent all the time—no matter what was happening around him.

Civic Government

The fourth area of authority that God has set up for us is our government. In America, our government is truly a blessing because it protects our right to worship God the way we want to, without fear of persecution. I'm thankful for our police officers, firefighters, city council members, mayor and our other local servants, who all work hard to ensure that we have the opportunity to work, worship and play in safety and freedom. I'm also thankful for our national government personnel, who serve us so diligently and work to make sure that we are protected and secure.

Romans 13 talks about government with clarity:

> Everyone must submit himself to the governing authorities, for there is no authority except that which God has established. The authorities that exist have been established by God. Consequently, he who rebels against the authority is rebelling against what God has instituted, and those who do so will bring judgment on themselves. For rulers hold no terror for those who do right, but for those who do wrong. Do you want to be free from fear of the one in authority? Then do what is right and he will commend you. For he is God's servant to do you good. But if you do wrong, be afraid, for he does not bear the sword for nothing. He is God's servant, an agent of wrath to bring punishment on the wrongdoer. Therefore, it is necessary to submit to the authorities, not only because of possible punishment but also because of conscience. This is also why you pay taxes, for the authorities are God's servants, who give their full time to governing. Give everyone what you owe him: If you owe taxes, pay taxes; if revenue, then revenue; if respect, then respect; if honor, then honor (vv. 1-7).

So, I don't break the law. I vote in elections. I respect those who win elections. If I inadvertently speed in my car and get caught, I don't fight with the officer about it. I pay the ticket and thank God that He had someone there to protect my life. When we build, we submit to the laws that apply to our structure, rather than trying to find ways around them. When I'm on an airplane, as I am right now, I cooperate with those who are in authority. I don't yell at ticket agents, I don't argue with flight attendants, I don't try to push the system, and it serves me well.

In his letter to young Timothy, Paul advised him to pray for governmental authority:

> I urge, then, first of all, that requests, prayers, intercession and thanksgiving be made for everyone—for kings and all those in authority, that we may live peaceful and quiet lives in all godliness and holiness. This is good, and pleases God our Savior, who wants all men to be saved and to come to a knowledge of the truth (1 Tim. 2:1-4).

Here, Paul is suggesting two reasons that it is important to pray for those in authority: so that we can practice our faith peacefully without infringement and so that God's kingdom may come stronger into the earth so that people may come to know Him.

As you go through life, you will be both under authority and in positions of authority. If you understand the biblical principles that guide both situations, you will succeed. God intended those in authority to protect and serve those under authority. He wants to bless people by rightly aligning them within these structures so they can experience great favor and success.

But what if there is abuse from authorities? Remember that God is our ultimate authority—always. The authority structures around us exist only because of God. So if they ever directly contradict God's Word, you must obey God's Word. If a parent ever demands that a child be immoral, the child should disobey the parents and obey the scriptural admonitions to live a moral life. If an employer ever asks employees to steal, they should disobey their employer and obey God's command not to steal. If a pastor ever uses his authority to ask people to do something shameful, they should disobey their pastor and obey the Word of God. If a government ever forbids the worship of God, citizens should disobey and worship according to the Scriptures.

I love the two of you so much. As you stay dressed and ready for the plan of God for your lives and apply these kingdom principles outlined in this letter, your lives will be incredibly protected, and you will have rich blessings flowing in your direction. God bless you! Do well!

I love being your dad,

REFLECTION AND DISCUSSION

1. Why is the tongue such a powerful tool?
2. What is the secret to honoring God's authority in the workplace?
3. Why is the local church so important in the life of an individual?
4. Paul suggests two reasons why it is important to pray for those in authority. What are they, and why?
5. What does the content of your thoughts have to do with your future?

Understand the Consequences of Your Beliefs

March 10

Dear Christy and Marcus,

I was tired when I got home on Thursday night, so after dinner Gayle, Jonathan, Alex, Elliott and I sat down to watch *Survivor*. While watching the show and munching on some popcorn, the phone rang. On the line was the daughter of one of the ladies in the church. Her voice was panicked. She screamed frantically into the phone that she thought her mother might be dead. She said that she was at the Penrose Hospital emergency room with her sisters and that they needed me to come right away. I left immediately.

When I arrived, the woman was unconscious and had been placed on a respirator to help her breathe. Three of her four daughters were there, and they were shaken, saddened and confused about their mother. They told me that the night before she had been fine, but when one of them arrived late that afternoon to take her to dinner, she found that her mom hadn't been able to get out of bed all day.

It's two days later now. The phone just rang a few moments ago as I sat down to write you this letter. It was one of the daughters. The doctors have told them that their mother has severe brain damage from lack of oxygen. Her chances of ever waking up are less than 1 percent.

Now the girls are faced with a dreadful decision—do they keep their mother on the respirator and hope for the best, or do they allow nature to take its course? They are conflicted about what to do. They know that their mother had always hoped to go to be with the Lord in her sleep, and that she looked forward to heaven very much. At times they wish they hadn't called the paramedics, so their mom could have gone to heaven from home; other times they have a faint hope that she'll recover, or at least wake up long enough for each of them to tell her how much they love her. Then they return to thinking that the best thing for her is to slip on into eternity, knowing that her love for the Lord is so strong.

All of the decisions they could make seem good; no one choice seems objectively better than the rest. The girls are caught in a dilemma, and it's nearly impossible for them to make a decision.

Fortunately, the girls aren't arguing about what to do. I've dealt with similar situations in other families where people disagreed so vehemently that they spent weeks after their loved one's death fighting with each other. Sometimes people have had their lawyers become involved, and relationships are wounded almost permanently.

Christy and Marcus, this highlights one of the great struggles in life: conflicting ways of thinking make life difficult. In the situation with these girls' mother, there are different theories that could be applied to reach a decision. Some would say that life must be maintained and preserved no matter what the cost and regardless of personal preference. Others would say that maintaining this woman on a life support system is neither her desire nor the desire of her family, and that she should be disconnected to allow nature to take its course. The girls are hearing the best of both theories and realizing that even the most well-reasoned opinions have dramatically different results.

As I've been explaining to you in these letters, beliefs have consequences. If you believe in concept A, you will make decisions according to concept A. If you believe in concept B, you will make different decisions. Both concept A and concept B could be well-articulated, reasonable ideas, but it's your decision to believe in one over the other that will determine your future course. Our beliefs impact the way we see the world and the way we live—sometimes even bringing division.

Some people who ride their horses English-style have an attitude about those who ride Western-style. Some snowboarders have strong opinions about skiers. People who believe that free markets are the best way to eliminate poverty usually anger people who believe in government programs for the redistribution of wealth. People who drive Fords sometimes don't like people who drive Chevys, and on and on.

Jesus said some things in Luke 12 that very few people talk about, some things that showed the powerful consequence of His teachings. He said,

> I have come to bring fire on the earth, and how I wish it were already kindled! But I have a baptism to undergo, and how distressed I am until it is completed! Do you think I came to bring peace on earth? No, I tell you, but division. From now on there will be five in one family divided against each other, three against two and two against three. They will be divided, father against son and son against father, mother against daughter and daughter against mother, mother-in-law against

daughter-in-law and daughter-in-law against mother-in-law (vv. 49-53).

Wow! Can you believe those words? Many people want to portray Jesus as a soft, gentle man who would never do anything very decisive. But when He turned the tables of the moneychangers over, He showed substance and resolve. When He healed a crippled man on the Sabbath in front of the Pharisees, right after they told Him it was unlawful to do so, He proved that He was bold enough to stick to His beliefs. And here, when He says that He did not come to bring peace but a sword, He shows that He knows that believing in something can sometimes cause division. Specifically, He says that believing in *Him* will cause division, even between family members.

I have seen Jesus' words come true here many times over the years. There are dads and moms in our church who come by themselves every Sunday morning because their families refuse to believe in Jesus. Some of the teens in our youth group have parents who refuse to support their decision to serve Christ. Not long ago, the president of a world missions organization spoke at our church and told us how his son disowned the family for years because he hated Christ and Christians. Fortunately, his son recently repented and gave his life to Christ, but for some people, believing in Christ creates divisions that last forever.

You see, Christy and Marcus, there is a consequence to believing anything. No matter what you like, what you believe or what you think, there is someone, somewhere, who will volunteer to be your enemy. When you choose to believe in something, the issue surfaces as to whether or not you are willing to deal with the ensuing conflicts. Can you stick by your beliefs no matter the consequences?

This is the next principle that will help you to live successful lives:

UNDERSTAND THE CONSEQUENCES OF YOUR BELIEFS.

This idea has really come alive to me in the last few years. I've had several people become my enemies simply because they disapprove of the friends I've chosen in ministry. As I considered the situation, it dawned on me that I would receive benefits and consequences for *every* position I took, so I need to consider my beliefs carefully and be then ready to stick to them.

Of course, belief in Jesus Christ will create all sorts of consequences. Being a Christian in the United States used to be honorable. But I remember realizing in high school that there were powerful forces in our nation working against the goodness of Christianity. That's why I committed my life to strengthening the Body of Christ. I knew that if we didn't focus on communicating His message well, things might become very difficult for Christians in America. And, indeed, things have become more and more difficult. Thankfully, we still enjoy freedom of religion and can worship without fear of government persecution. But Christians have begun to be persecuted in this country in other ways.

Recently, Thomas Horn wrote an article describing how Christians are being persecuted in the United States. Consider the following:

More Christians died for their faith in the twentieth century than at any other time in history, says Christian

Solidarity International. Global reports indicate that over 150,000 Christians were martyred last year, chiefly outside of the United States. However, statistics are changing: Persecution of Christians is on the increase in the United States. What's happening to bring about this change?

According to some experts, a pattern is emerging reminiscent of Jewish persecution in post war Germany. "Isolation of, and discrimination against, Christians is growing almost geometrically," says Don McAlvany in *The Midnight Herald*. "This is the way it started in Germany against the Jews. As they became more isolated and marginalized by the Nazi propaganda machine, as popular hatred and prejudice against the Jews increased among the German people, wholesale persecution followed. Could this be where the growing anti-Christian consensus in America is taking us?"

Tolerance of anti-Christian attitudes in the United States is escalating. Recently, a woman in Houston, Texas, was ordered by local police to stop handing out gospel tracts to children who knocked on her door during Halloween. Officers informed her that such activity is illegal (not true), and that she would be arrested if she continued. In Madison, Wisconsin, the Freedom from Religion Foundation distributes anti-Christian pamphlets to public school children entitled, "We Can Be Good Without God." The entertainment industry and syndicated media increasingly vilify Christians as sewer rats, vultures and simpleminded social ingrates. The FBI and the Clinton White House brand fundamentalist Christian groups as hate mongers and potential terrorists. The Council of Religious Leaders of Metropolitan Chicago warns that plans by Southern Baptists to hold a convention in the Windy City next year might foment "hate crimes" against minorities, causing some Christians to fear that speaking openly about their religious beliefs will soon be considered a crime. All this, while Christianity itself is often a target of hate-crime violence. We remember the students at Columbine and the United Methodist minister who was fatally beaten and burned in a remote part of Chattanooga, Tennessee, to name a few of the recent examples of interpersonal violence aimed at believers.[1]

Christy and Marcus, I'm not highlighting these things to frighten you, but to help you understand that believing in the gospel sets you apart. It makes you different, and as you go through life as strong Christians, certain groups of people won't understand why you believe the way you do. Many people will feel threatened by your beliefs. At times, being a Christian may mean that you are ostracized, verbally abused or even physically persecuted. The gospel divides groups of people. Since you two are chosen by God to do great things, you are in the company of great people, but it carries a price.

I hear people say from time to time that they know God's will by following peace. Don't do this! I don't believe it. You know God's will by obeying the Scriptures, fellowshiping in the Holy Spirit and honoring your authorities. Every great character in the Bible had to do the hard thing in order to achieve the calling of God on his or her life. I doubt that Gideon was thrilled about spying on and fighting against the Midianites. I doubt that Jesus felt peace in the Garden of Gethsemene. I doubt that Paul enjoyed being beaten, and I doubt that David was smiling and laughing about his battle with Goliath.

Believing in something—even the gospel—doesn't mean that life will be easy. In fact, in some parts of the world, it means just the opposite. We all hear stories about how the early Christians were persecuted by Roman officials, but Christians are being persecuted today, too. As Horn's article mentions, more Christians suffered persecution in the twentieth century than in any other time in history.

International Christian Concern (an organization addressing Christian persecution profiles by region and by country for countries where there is known persecution) published a couple of reports of some recent activity in Indonesia, China and Cuba that I think are important for you to look at. I've copied some portions of the reports below.[2] Christy and Marcus, please read over these slowly and carefully. This describes what is happening to Christians all over the globe on a daily basis. This information is tragic and horrifying, but I want you to be fully aware of the consequences some people have had to pay for their belief in Christ.

Indonesia

- Violence between Muslims and Christians began on January 19, 1999, during a dispute between a Christian bus driver and a Muslim passenger. Insiders say, however, that the incident simply provided the necessary catalyst for militant Muslims to instigate a premeditated plan of violence against Christians. As of February of 2001, an estimated 8,000 people have been killed in the resulting violence and at least 500,000 have been displaced.
- January 10, 2001: A carful of Christians was attacked as it traveled through the Muslim neighborhood of Galunggung in Ambon. Three were wounded and two remain missing as a result of the attack. Two other Christians were seriously wounded in Batumerah when their limousine was shot at.
- December 24, 2000: Several churches were destroyed and at least 19 people were killed as bombs exploded in

or near Christian churches all over the country. Several Catholic churches in Jakarta were targeted as well as churches in West Java, Batam Island and Sumatra. By God's grace many other bombs were discovered before they were able to detonate.

- December 1, 2000: On Kasiui Island, teachers David Balubun and E. Rumatera were beheaded for refusing to convert to Islam.
- September 26, 2000: Muslim men clad in white fired mortars on Christians in Hative Besar, killing at least five people and razing nearly 60 homes. Suli and Galala villages were also attacked by members of neighboring villages.
- June 19-20, 2000: Between 160 and 180 Christians were killed when a large force of Muslim fighters attacked Duma on the island of Halmahera. Another 20 to 30 women and children were carried off by the attackers and are assumed dead. Around 300 homes are destroyed.

China

- More than 400 private homes serving as places of worship for Christians were destroyed in the months of November and December. Not only is the non-Christian Falun Gong targeted for annihilation and considered a "foreign devil," but Christians also. If a pastor of one these house churches is found without registration, he or she is jailed and his or her home destroyed.

Cuba

- September 26, 2000: While a Christian pastor and his wife were traveling, Cuban authorities entered their house and threw all of the family's belongings into the street. Jorge Ferrer's father and two children were also evicted from the house. The family was not allowed to reenter their home, which was evidently taken from them because it had been used for Christian meetings. Members of the Ferrers' church held a prayer vigil outside of the house, but it has not been restored to the family as of yet.

- October 8, 1999: Osmany Dominguez Borjas, pastor of the United Pentecostal Church in Havana, was arrested for holding an evangelical celebration.
- February 1999: Thousands of Bibles, printed in the U.S., were seized by security forces and burned near the military unit Arroyo Naranjo near Managua, as they were considered subversive.
- October 9, 1998: Ester Nieto Collazo was strangled in her home. She had apparently been raped and had suffered physical abuse. Ester was the executive secretary at the Evangelical League of Cuba, where her husband and brother also worked. Ester's brother, Alejandro Nieto, pastors the church and had faced frequent harassment from the government for his evangelistic activities and his unwillingness to abide by the restrictive religious laws.

I am conflicted as I write this to you, because I don't want to discourage you in your faith. But I would be a dishonorable father if I didn't adequately prepare you for the realities of this present evil age.

You are called to be light and to be salt. What you believe will have profound consequences that affect your life and future. This is not a cause for fear, but for great hope! Your generation can make the world a better place. You are called to invest your lives in persuading others. Do it powerfully. Do it for the kingdom of God. Do it well. It is well worth facing the consequences.

I am so pleased with you.

I love being your dad,

REFLECTION AND DISCUSSION

1. What is the problem with believing in something?
2. How do ideas, even good ideas, divide us?
3. How did reading the stories about what contemporary Christians are going through make you feel?
4. How does believing in the gospel set you apart?
5. Name three ways to know God's will.

Notes
1. Thomas Horn, "Persecution of Christians Growing the U.S.," *OpinioNet*, December 7, 2000. http://www.OpinioNet.com (no access date).
2. These reports and other information regarding the persecution of Christians can be obtained through International Christian Concern's website at http://www.persecution.org.

DISCERN THE TIMES

March 13

Dear Christy and Marcus,

> When you see a cloud rising in the west, immediately you say, "It's going to rain," and it does. And when the south wind blows, you say, "It's going to be hot," and it is. Hypocrites! You know how to interpret the appearance of the earth and the sky. How is it that you don't know how to interpret this present times? (Luke 12:54-56).

Why is Jesus rebuking these guys? Because they claimed to be informed, yet didn't understand their own moment in history. They recognized some things *about* their world, but overlooked the most important thing: what God was doing *in* their world.

Every one of us needs to be aware of where we are in space and time. We need to know our physical context (where we are geographically, and what that means for us) and our historical context (where we are historically, and what that means for us). Think of the tragedy if Winston Churchill had not known how important it was that the Allies prevail during World War II. What if Martin Luther King, Jr., had missed his moment in history as a crusader for civil rights? Or if Abraham Lincoln had loved pacifying people more than fighting for principles of freedom? What if our founding fathers had decided that it was easier to be subject to England than to be free? If any of these people hadn't been aware of where they were in time, their misjudgments could have altered history in terrible ways. In my mind, they are models of the next principle of successful living:

DISCERN THE TIMES.

Unfortunately, some people are remembered primarily for their inability to discern their time:

- Charles Duell, the Commissioner of the U.S. Office of Patents in 1899, said: "Everything that can be invented, has been invented."
- The men who dug water wells in the nineteenth century resisted Edwin Drake's progressive idea that oil could be found below the earth's surface as well as water. "You want us to drill into the ground to find oil?" they asked. "You're crazy!"
- In 1927, H.M. Warner of Warner Brothers argued that there was no need to add sound to movies. "Who the heck wants to hear actors talk?" he exclaimed.
- In 1962, Decca Recording rejected the Beatles, saying, "We don't like their sound, and guitar music is on the way out." (Which is probably why you've never heard of Decca Recording!)
- In 1977, Ken Olson, president, chairman and founder of Digital Equipment Corporation, said, "There is no reason anyone would want a computer in their home."

These people didn't rightly discern the times in which they lived. Because of it, they missed some incredible opportunities.

I believe that this is something Christians desperately need to get right. We need to know:

1. What God is doing in our generation
2. What our role is in His plan

Bible scholars and historians have concluded that because Jesus came when Rome ruled the world, the gospel was able to spread into a global religion with greater ease. Many believe that God chose for Jesus to come to Earth during that time because He knew that the geopolitical situation could be used to fulfill His plans.

I think this hour is the same. I think God has chosen this time for the most aggressive expansion of the kingdom of God in history.

More people are coming to Christ on a daily basis than ever before in history. More people are experiencing miracles and witnessing the power of God than ever before. There are more Christians in the world than at any other point in history, and there are more Christians in America right now than at any other point in history.

You are both citizens of one of the most powerful nations on Earth. Because of this, there are very few countries to which it would be difficult for you to travel, and very few countries that would be financially difficult for you to impact. The world has more wealth than ever before, more democratically elected governments than ever before and more countries embracing the wealth-creating power of free markets than ever before. Many are also embracing the ideologies that coincide with the free market system—freedom of religion, speech and press. These current geopolitical situations also serve to ease the spread of the gospel by giving us the resources needed to bring God's message to the nations.

The Christian community is also more united than it has been since the Reformation. Protestants work together more, strategize together more and share resources more. What does that mean? It means if you'll look around and see what God is doing and devote yourselves to His plan, you'll have unlimited opportunity.

But if we don't accurately discern what God is doing on the earth and what our role is in it, we will fall short of our maximum potential. So, once we commit our lives to God and His kingdom work, we have to be sure that we're not distracted.

I think there are two major mistakes young Christian men and women make in their thinking which have the potential to throw their lives off course. One is misunderstanding where they are in end-time events; the other is misunderstanding the importance of a strong education.

All my life I've been hearing that Jesus would be returning soon. When I was your age, we were in the middle of the Jesus Movement. Part of the fervor of that movement was fueled by a book entitled *The Late Great Planet Earth*, about the imminent return of Jesus. I haven't read it for years, but I remember this book circulating through my high school and loads of kids getting saved and renewing their interest in Christ because of it. At the same time, there were movies like *A Thief in the Night* and others that depicted current events as the final fulfillment of biblical prophecy, "proving" that the Second Coming of Christ was near.

All of this convinced some people that Jesus was going to return any minute. Because they felt that the world was about to end, they began making drastic decisions. Some of my friends married girls that they really didn't want to spend their lives with, because they wanted to be married for a while before Jesus returned. Others avoided college because they were convinced that Jesus would return before they could finish their education.

The excitement about the Second Coming saturated Christian culture. Much of our study, cultural engagement (the arts, etc.) and ministry focused on expanding the kingdom of God before His return. So we had a wonderful motivation for evangelism. But years passed, and He didn't come. And, as you know, He still hasn't.

As you might imagine, many of those high school friends of mine who were influenced simply by the fervor of the day and didn't rightly discern the times became disillusioned. Some of them are no longer involved with the Church because their trust in Christian leadership was shattered. They felt they were deceived by people using fear tactics simply to sell books and movies. In my opinion, though, this really wasn't the case. All of the people I knew who were promoting those ideas were trying to help their readers and viewers develop a deep, personal dependency on God through Bible reading and prayer. They weren't asking people to make rash, impulsive decisions—they were just trying to get them dressed and ready to serve God. The listeners came to God for the wrong reasons and ended up making serious mistakes.

This has gone on in the Church for some time. Your great-grandmother Gossard lived outside Altamont, Kansas, at the turn of the nineteenth century. In that day, it was well accepted among many Christians that Jesus was going to return at midnight on December 31, 1899. On New Year's Eve, a few farmers released their cattle, turned their pigs loose and gave away their farm machinery. Some signed over titles of their land to non-Christians.

As the clock inched toward the stroke of midnight, some of my grandmother's neighbors wrapped themselves in white sheets and sat on top of their barns to wait. Of course, we know what happened—nothing!

On January 1, 1900, there was a lot of scrambling going on because people didn't accurately assess the times. They were foolish in their interpretation of the Bible and misguided in the way they interpreted the times. They missed it.

Unfortunately, the same thing is happening today. Many people in our generation are missing it too. As a family we heard the uproar when the clock passed into January 1, 2000. "Respected" prophets had foretold all sorts of disasters, and Bible "scholars" had made a fortune selling books and tapes predicting the end of the age. As you remember, at New Life we decided to subtly spite them all and have a wedding/New Year's celebration on December 31, 1999. While we were having a great party, many people were wasting their time and resources on what amounted to a hoax.

This is not to poke fun at those who wanted to be prepared, but to emphasize that to rightly discern the times we must stay true to the Word: The Bible says that Jesus will return and that we need to be about Kingdom business until then. It also makes a clear case that our focus should not be on when (see Matt. 24: 3-5,11). It's clear that Jesus knew a cloud of confusion would surround people's fascination with the end times, but many seemed to have missed His warning. When we fail to hear the Word of God we are bound to become distracted from His true purposes.

When Jesus didn't come back after the uproar caused by the Jesus Movement, I started studying for myself what the Bible had to say about Jesus' Second Coming. Right away, it was clear that people, wanting to prove that Jesus was coming back at that time, altered the meanings of words, extrapolated their own ideas from symbols in the Bible and did a poor job of interpreting current events.

For example, when I was in high school, people said that Jesus had to return to Earth before the nation of Israel turned 40 years old. He didn't. Then they said He had to return within 40 years of Israel's control of Jerusalem. He didn't. Now they are saying the number 40 should have been 70. This is too much for me. I don't think we can keep changing the rules.

They also said that there would be a great falling away from the Church before the Second Coming, and they pointed to the rise in cults to demonstrate that this great falling away was happening. Well, now that I'm old enough to be personal friends with some of the world's most renowned missiologists, I've learned that in the last 40 years, we've not seen a falling away at all. Instead, we've seen a rapid expansion of God's power and revival. We are seeing the opposite of a great falling away. We are living in the generation of the great ingathering.

They also said that the United Nations was proof that the Second Coming was near because of the one-world government that is necessary for the work of the Antichrist. Well, no doubt the United Nations could become that one-world government if a global crisis struck. But right now, the United Nations is not a one-world government; in fact, they are without the military and economic strength of the United States. Another teaching was that the first leader of this global government would be evil. Yet, from what I read in the Bible, the world might prosper for hundreds of years under global economic and governmental control before the Antichrist takes his position in that system. We're not there yet.

They pointed to earthquakes and natural disasters and told people that these things were proof that the Second Coming was near. Well, from what I read in Matthew 24:7-8, Jesus says that these are the beginnings of birth pangs. In other words, they are indeed an indicator—of the *beginning* of the end. People are jumping the gun and distracting their audiences from more important work.

Another indicator some pointed to as a sure sign of Christ's return was the rebuilding of the Temple in Jerusalem. I had been told that there were plans to rebuild the Temple on the temple mount in Jerusalem, that animals were being prepared for sacrifices to God and that other specific preparations were being made. This was important because many believed that the "abomination that causes desolation" (Matt. 24:15) had to occur in the Temple. Well, I've learned since that there are no current plans by responsible people for the construction on the temple mount, nor are there animals being prepared by people of influence. And the "abomination that causes desolation" is open to a great variety of interpretations that do not necessarily point to the Temple in Jerusalem. Thus, after going back to the Word, I don't think this is a credible indicator.

So after saying all of that, where are we in the end times? We are in Matthew 24:14, which says, "And this gospel of the kingdom will be preached in the whole world as a testimony to all nations, and then the end will come." Right now, God is building the greatest body of churches the world has ever seen. They teach people to be born again and spirit filled and instruct people to read the Bible and consume its principles. Most of these great churches are outreach churches, which means they are reaching into the community of people who do not know the Lord and are helping them find Christ.

Marcus, remember when you and I went to Seoul, South Korea, for the Global Consultation on World Evangelization? That meeting marked the first time we as a Church had quantified the remaining task of the Great Commission. Jesus said in Matthew 28:

> All authority in heaven and on earth has been given to me. Therefore go and make disciples of all nations, baptizing them in the name of the Father and of the Son and of the Holy Spirit, and teaching them to obey everything I have commanded you. And surely I am with you

always, to the very end of the age (vv. 18-20).

He gave us this commission 2000 years ago, and since that meeting in 1995, we have had an accurate list of the unreached people groups of the world, the least-evangelized people groups and the areas of the world where the gospel is available. In other words, we know how much there is left to do. We know where the people are who do not currently have the gospel available to them, we know the languages they speak, and we are mobilizing churches and servant ministries to strategically serve these people, so they can have the opportunity to know Christ.

This is the calling of your generation. This is what the Lord is doing. And if you will use your resources and not become distracted with false hopes of a premature Second Coming or paralyzed by self-absorption, but instead be consumed with His purposes in this time, you will perfectly fulfill the reason God created you. This is for *you*. This is your purpose. This is what God is doing in this generation.

To be effective in this calling, it is very important that you aggressively secure a strong education. Education is all about ideas, and while you are getting your education, you will be exposed to good ideas and bad ideas. You will be exposed to a variety of ideas and cultures. You will need to filter those thoughts through the Word of God and God's work in your generation, so you can be a strong voice for His kingdom. Without education you might not have the skills you'll need to reach people with God's message. Your sphere of influence could be unnecessarily limited.

There are voices in our Christian culture which discourage getting a strong education. I think those voices are wrong; they limit some of our best young men and women. They will try and tell you that you don't need an education because the anointing of the Holy Spirit is enough, because natural gifting is enough. Or they will encourage you to displace the responsibility to reach your generation by telling you that God will supernaturally and solitarily build His ministry.

Well, those things sound great and are true to a point. But I think we are responsible to prepare ourselves and to be well aware of where the world is, what it is thinking and what it takes to influence it.

The most influential person in the Old Testament was well educated. In Acts 7:22, the Bible says, "Moses was educated in all the wisdom of the Egyptians and was powerful in speech and action." Moses had the best education in the world as an adopted son of Pharaoh—the most powerful man in the world at the time. Moses understood the current thought of the day and was well-informed and well-read. He had a wonderful encounter with God, and because of his background and relationships, he had access to Pharaoh and was able to confront his generation and become the most influential personality in the Old Testament.

The second most influential person in the Old Testament was King David. He understood government, power, war, God, economics, music and architecture—to name a few. He wrote prose and poetry and was a dynamic leader and persuasive speaker. He was extremely well educated.

In the New Testament, the primary personality is Jesus Christ. The Bible is virtually silent on Jesus' early years with the exception of one incident that tells us a great deal about what He was like as a child. In Luke 2, the Bible says:

> Every year his parents went to Jerusalem for the Feast of the Passover. When he was twelve years old, they went up to the Feast, according to the custom. After the Feast was over, while his parents were returning home, the boy Jesus stayed behind in Jerusalem, but they were unaware

of it. Thinking he was in their company, they traveled on for a day. Then they began looking for him among their relatives and friends. When they did not find him, they went back to Jerusalem to look for him. After three days they found him in the temple courts, sitting among the teachers, listening to them and asking them questions. Everyone who heard him was amazed at his understand ing and his answers. When his parents saw him, they were astonished. His mother said to him, "Son, why have you treated us like this? Your father and I have been anxiously searching for you."

"Why were you searching for me?" he asked. "Didn't you know I had to be in my Father's house?" But they did not understand what he was saying to them.

Then he went down to Nazareth with them and was obedient to them. But his mother treasured all these things in her heart. And Jesus grew in wisdom and stature, and in favor with God and men (vv. 41-52).

Jesus was thinking and was engaging in thought with the most notable leaders of his day. The last paragraph points out that Jesus maintained virtue while growing and learning; He was obedient to His parents, and He grew in wisdom as He grew in stature, and He grew in favor with God and men. In other words, He became well aware of what was going on around Him. He was well educated. He humbled Himself to become a student.

All the great people I know are great because they were great students. Throughout the ministry of Christ, it is evident that He was well-informed about the religious and political situations surrounding His life and ministry. He did not live in a vacuum. Instead, He was active and able to engage people both spiritually and intellectually. He understood ideas. *Ideas* . . . ideas are what education is all about.

The second most powerful personality in the New Testament is the apostle Paul. Paul was a Pharisee, just like his father (Pharisees were some of the best-educated men in Israel). They knew and loved the Law. They dominated the Sanhedrin, which was the highest court and legislative body of the Jews during Jesus' day. Paul was a Roman citizen, which meant he was from a well-respected family. In Galatians 1:14, he communicated his proficiency in education when he said: "I was advancing in Judaism beyond many Jews of my own age and was extremely zealous for the traditions of my fathers." He was well educated and became skilled in many areas. He was successful in business, so much so that he was able to finance most of his own missionary activities. He was a skilled and thoughtful speaker, and God used his skills and abilities in a powerful way. Paul wrote two-thirds of the New Testament and was used to open the door for Christianity to become more than a simple Jewish sect, but a world-changing influence.

Christy and Marcus, aggressively pursue your education. Get your bachelor's degrees as early in life as you possibly can. Then you can get your master's degrees or doctorates whenever you would like, if ever. But I believe that a bachelor's degree from an accredited university positions you to lead like a high school education did only one generation ago. Here at New Life Church, we won't hire anyone in a salaried position unless he or she has a bachelor's degree. Why? Because we want people who have been through the experience of learning in a formal environment. It's very important.

So what should you do? How can you get a strong education and maintain a strong spiritual life as well? Either attend a well-respected Christian university or take one year to study the Bible and be discipled at some point during your undergraduate education. That way, you can get the best of both worlds. That's why we offer the Route 24/7 intern program here at

New Life. It's designed for young men and women who are pursuing their bachelor's degree to take a year of concentrated discipleship, so they can be healthy, well-informed leaders.

As I wrote to you earlier, it is said that the last century was dominated by the lives of seven men: Lenin, Stalin, Hitler, Mao Tse-tung, Roosevelt, Churchill and Reagan. All of these men were committed to a set of ideas. Four of the seven were committed to ideas that ended up costing millions of people their freedom and their lives, but three were committed to a set of ideas that helped people and led to the freedom and prosperity that you are enjoying today. Since you are called to impact society and the world and to make life better for people, you have to be able to work with ideas and persuade others. All of these men were committed thinkers, and all of them were able to persuade and inspire others. They gained the right to be heard, and they changed the world.

You are called to change the world, too.

If you are not in the mix of persuading and fighting for good ideas, bad ideas will prevail. If Roosevelt, Churchill and Reagan hadn't entered the competition of ideas, we could very easily have lost civilization as we know it.

Strong believers need to be able to participate well in the marketplace of ideas. Strong Christians need to be on every school board, in every classroom, in every legal case, on every Supreme Court and in every business. We need strong Christians writing television programs for the major networks and movies for the major studios. We need strong Christians as major athletes and the superstars of your generation. Christians are salt and light, and we need to be everywhere, serving humanity and encouraging humanity to be more humane.

That's why it's important to know what God is doing in this generation and what your role in His plan is. That's why you need to know that this generation's call is to reach into every person's world and touch them with the life of Christ, which requires "growing in favor with God and man." As you do this, you will be the people God can use to make the world a better place.

I love being your dad,

REFLECTION AND DISCUSSION

1. Think of some other people in history or who are alive today that correctly discerned the times. What can you learn from them?
2. How can you avoid the two major mistakes young people make that throw their lives off course?
3. What do you need to know to correctly discern the times and maximize your potential? Do you know those things already, or do you need to learn them?
4. Why is education so crucial to your calling?
5. Why is it important for Christians to be everywhere in the marketplace of ideas?

LEARN TO MANAGE CONFLICT

March 19

Dear Christy and Marcus,

Last night after church I met with three people. The first one was a man who was trying to assess what he ought to do with his friend who had recently had an affair and was preparing to leave his wife. The second was a woman who had had an affair with a man, thinking that he would leave his wife for her, but he didn't. Now she has to decide what to do. The third person was a young man who has been married less than two years and now knows that he doesn't love his wife and that his wife doesn't love him.

In each of these cases, the emotions running amuck are destroying families and relationships. And all of these people had two things in common: They were dominated by mismanaged affection, and they were trying to predict how others were going to react to their decisions. How would people feel about them? Would they be accepted or rejected?

This issue is huge; in fact, it's one of the principle issues in life. Every day, we have to deal with how people feel about us and how we feel about other people. I've seen the two of you deal with it many times. I've watched both of you respond positively to the approval of a teacher or a friend, and I've seen you have to decide what to do when a teacher or a friend was not as approving as you would have liked.

Our emotions, hearts and thoughts can so easily become confused when we're focused on other people's feelings about us. In general, we want to be accepted by everyone and we try to avoid conflict with others. But, like it or not, conflict is going to happen. Emotions will flair up and feelings will be hurt. Inevitably, we are going to say or do things—intentionally or not—that hurt others, and people are going to say or do things that cause us hurt. We need to know how to navigate the meaning of these feelings and determine how they will impact our lives.

Thus, the last principle of healthy living that I want to share with you is this:

LEARN TO MANAGE CONFLICT.

This is precisely what Jesus is talking about in the last section of Luke 12.

> Why don't you judge for yourselves what is right? As you are going with your adversary to the magistrate, try hard to be reconciled to him on the way, or he may drag you off to the judge, and the judge turn you over to the officer, and the officer throw you into prison. I tell you, you will not get out until you have paid the last penny (vv. 57-59).

Here, Jesus is talking about two people who have hurt each other so much that they've created a case for the courts. Both parties feel they are right and they are seeking justice.

It's always interested me that Jesus never promises justice through courts. He always encourages people to settle their issues outside of court. Paul addressed this subject the same way, saying:

> If any of you has a dispute with another, dare he take it before the ungodly for judgment instead of before the saints? Do you not know that the saints will judge the world? And if you are to judge the world, are you not competent to judge trivial cases? Do you not know that we will judge angels? How much more the things of this life! Therefore, if you have disputes about such matters, appoint as judges even men of little account in the church! I say this to shame you. Is it possible that there is nobody among you wise enough to judge a dispute between believers? But instead, one brother goes to law against another—and this in front of unbelievers! The very fact that you have lawsuits among you means you have been completely defeated already. Why not rather be wronged? Why not rather be cheated? Instead, you yourselves cheat and do wrong, and you do this to your brothers (1 Cor. 6:1-8).

Neither Jesus nor Paul says that justice is the goal. And neither encourages us to take revenge or punish people who have done wrong things to us or have betrayed us in some way. They both say just the opposite: Work for reconciliation. Paul even says it is better to be wronged than to try to find remedy to a problem in the courts.

The point: It is the condition of our heart that matters, not whether we are right or wrong. Whether we are accepted or rejected by others, we need to stay innocent and clean before God.

This is the prayer Jesus taught us: "Forgive us our debts, as we also have forgiven our debtors" (Matt. 6:12). He explained by saying:

> For if you forgive men when they sin against you, your heavenly Father will also forgive you. But if you do not forgive men their sins, your Father will not forgive your sins (vv. 14-15).

Since God has forgiven us so graciously, we have an obligation to treat others the same way. If we don't, God's forgiveness is no longer available to us.

The other day I went to the Red Robin to have lunch with a group of friends, and I arrived a little early. While I was waiting, a lady and her daughter recognized me and came up to talk with me about a situation in their lives. As they described it, it was clear that their offender had gone on with his life, but they were still hurt and actually seething in anger and pain for what this man had done to them. It was obvious that they were being held hostage by their hatred against this person. They wanted justice.

I explained to them that justice was not going to come their way. What they needed to do was forgive. Then, after their hearts were clean, if they wanted to approach the man and try to work through the offense, that was fine. But in their current condition, they wanted to punish him, which was leaving them with hard hearts and angry spirits.

Christy and Marcus, right and wrong do not apply to forgiveness. Sure, there will be times when you are truly wronged, and you will feel like you have a right to be angry and hold a grudge. But God says not to do it. He wants you to be free from the burden of blaming others so that your heart can be open to accept His forgiveness toward you.

Several years ago a woman in another local church began spreading vicious, untrue rumors about me. She was connected to some key people, and soon her gossip was all over town. The effects were far-reaching, and the rumors began to have a negative impact on my entire ministry.

This woman was always sweet and cordial to me personally, but when I was absent, she slandered my life and work. I was so frustrated, and I debated within myself about how to confront the situation. After a while, I knew that I couldn't do anything until I got my heart clean. So, for a few weeks, each morning I rose early from bed and went for a long walk, verbally expressing to God my forgiveness toward this woman.

All this time, her stories grew more severe, and I became deeply offended. I didn't *feel* forgiving to her, but I kept surrendering it to God, telling Him that I forgave her anyway, trusting that He would correct my heart.

And He did. One night, God dropped genuine forgiveness into my heart. By His grace, I actually loved that woman. What is more, I was no longer emotionally connected to what she said. The rumors didn't phase me. I was ready to talk with her whenever God opened the door, but I wasn't concerned about her anymore. Amazingly, after I came to this perspective, I never even had to talk to her about the whole ordeal. God took care of it. To this day I haven't heard one more wicked word from her.

Matthew 5:44 says: "Love your enemies and pray for those who persecute you." You've heard that verse a thousand times, I'm sure, but think for a moment about what it means. Fortunately, the two of you have never had anyone declare themselves your enemy, but this was coming from the perspective of Jesus, who was surrounded by people who harbored a vile and desperate hatred of Him. They wanted Him dead and He knew it—but loved them powerfully anyway.

Can you imagine that? What if someone was out to make life miserable for you? What if they drained your finances and wreaked havoc on your relationships? I hope that never happens to either of you, but understand that it is that kind of person God is asking us to love. Paul wrote in his letter to the Romans: "If your enemy is hungry, feed him; if he is thirsty, give him something to drink. In doing this, you will heap burning coals on his head" (12:20). "Burning coals" would have been considered a blessing in Paul's day: Fire was an important commodity, and it was sometimes transported in containers filled with hot coals that people carried on their heads. Thus, a bucket of burning coals was a valuable gift, a demonstration of love. So, in other words, God is telling us that if someone hates you, take care of them. Love them and demonstrate your love.

Christy and Marcus, from the perspective of some people who don't know Christ, these ideas may sound foolish. As you go through life walking in forgiveness, you will undoubtedly have people telling you that you are letting people walk all over you. But what they won't understand is that because you are a Christian, you are free to let God handle judging other people for their actions—even when those actions are against you.

Paul told the Romans, "Do not take revenge, my friends, but leave room for God's wrath, for it is written: 'It is mine to avenge; I will repay,' says the Lord" (12:19). And in Proverbs 20:22 we read, "Do not say, 'I'll pay you back for this wrong!' Wait for the LORD, and he will deliver you." God is big and powerful, Christy and Marcus, and we need to trust Him to be the Judge of all. Let Him take care of other people: Just serve Him and others faithfully, and keep your heart innocent before Him.

While practicing keeping your heart clean, there is something else you'll need to understand in order to manage conflict: your role in every situation. In my ninth letter to you, I explained the four sets of authorities God has established here on the earth (the family, the church, the workplace and the government). When you have been violated, you must forgive. Once you've forgiven, if there needs to be some correction, then you can work within the chains of command that God has established.

If there is a problem in the family among siblings, the older the sibling the greater the responsibility he or she has to maintain order and provide justice to the younger members of the family. All of the siblings can look to parents, and between the parents, wives look to husbands. When a problem arises, after you ensure that your heart is clean, you should appeal to an older sibling or a parent to help resolve the conflict.

The workplace works in a similar way. Everyone has a boss, and even the owner of the company has to be responsible to the public they serve. If there is a problem at work, start by talking to the one with whom the problem originates. If that doesn't solve it, and the problem is significant enough to pursue, start working up the chain of command. When you do this, it will force your superiors to make a decision, so be wise: The decision might be sympathetic with your position, but it might be sympathetic with the person you are complaining about.

Over the years, a few church employees have come to me with ultimatums related to conflicts. Someone had a problem with another employee, and they were so convinced that they were right and that the other person (or persons) as wrong, that they actually threatened to resign if I didn't agree with their perspective. I find these types of demands to be absurd. When people do this, I am compelled to accommodate their absurdity and accept their resignation. If you cannot work out your conflicts in the early phases of the chain of command, and you feel strongly about seeking resolution, approach your authorities with an attitude of humility and respect and be prepared to be humbled before your adversary.

As for churches, which are the third system of order, the chain of command may work a little differently because church governments vary widely. But every church has some form of government, and within each government, responsibilities are spread out among the congregation, the senior pastor, the overseers and the board of trustees. Everyone is somehow responsible to someone else, so integrity and a high quality of work are maintained. Depending on your role in your church, you'll know who to contact to resolve conflict. Always remember that it's vital for you to observe the chain of command, stay within your role and honor the authorities that God has established.

It's also important to follow the chain of command in civil government. Fortunately, in America our government is set up efficiently enough that we generally know who to go to when there is a problem we need to deal with. Sometimes people get too upset about something and try to trump everyone's position by going to the highest power. But if you write the president of the United States a letter of complaint because you received an unfair traffic ticket, you aren't going to get very far. This is why it's important to make sure that your heart is clean first; then you can think clearly and carefully about the best way to resolve the conflict.

So, how do you solve problems with other people? Forgive the violation, and be sure that your heart is clean. Then, if necessary, use the appropriate chain of command to try to find resolution. But remember, it's better to settle the issue on the way, because God doesn't guarantee justice through these structures of order.

Christy and Marcus, I think these 12 letters contain some of the most wonderful secrets of life revealed in the Scriptures. I've written them so that you can keep them and review them from time to time. Each letter includes life principles that will serve you in an increasingly powerful way as you go through the years.

And I know that if you will apply them early and often, they will open the door for God's rich blessing on all of your life.

I love you very much and I want you to enjoy the riches of His blessing. My love for you, and my belief in you, are deep and strong. I know that you will be incredibly successful. I already see His favor on your life.

I love being your dad,

REFLECTION AND DISCUSSION

1. Why do you think it is important to God that believers settle their disputes outside of the courts?
2. What is the difference between reconciliation and justice?
3. How do you maintain an innocent, clean heart in the midst of persecution?
4. What is the role of forgiveness in managing conflict?

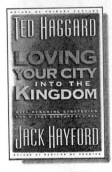